Notes for the Everlost

Notes for the Everlost

A Field Guide to Grief

*

Kate Inglis

Shambhala
Boulder
2018

Shambhala Publications, Inc.
4720 Walnut Street
Boulder, Colorado 80301
www.shambhala.com

9 8 7 6 5 4 3 2 1

First Edition
Printed in the United States of America

⊛ This edition is printed on acid-free paper that meets the
American National Standards Institute Z39.48 Standard.
♻ This book is printed on 30% postconsumer recycled paper.
For more information please visit www.shambhala.com.

Shambhala Publications is distributed worldwide by
Penguin Random House, Inc., and its subsidiaries.

Designed by Gopa & Ted2, Inc.

Library of Congress Cataloging-in-Publication Data
Names: Inglis, Kate, 1973– author.
Title: Notes for the everlost: a field guide to grief/Kate Inglis.
Description: First edition. | Boulder: Shambhala, 2018.
Identifiers: LCCN 2017028622 |
ISBN 9781611805505 (paperback: alkaline paper)
Subjects: LCSH: Inglis, Kate, 1973– | Parental grief. | Premature
Infants—Death. | Twins—Death. | Mother and child. |
Motherhood—Psychological aspects. | Mothers—Canada
—Biography. | Women
authors, Canadian—Biography.
Classification: LCC BF575.G7 I54 2018 | DDC 155.6/463—dc23
LC record available at https://lccn.loc.gov/2017028622

For bereaved parents
and for all those who find themselves here too, in what
feels like an everlost: this state, sentence, riddle, dream.
It is indelible until it fades, softly. That is what this book
is about, with the grief of infant loss serving as
the container to contemplate life, after.

I do not propose to write an ode to dejection, but to brag as lustily as chanticleer in the morning, standing on his roost, if only to wake my neighbors up.

—Henry David Thoreau, *Walden*

Contents

Introduction

C HARLIE CHAPLIN tiptoes inside the cage of a sleeping lion.
Oh, precarious life! Always danger, always little daisies.
Circus tightropes, gold rush bears, fire-swallowers. We love the
underdog because we like that even those who wouldn't think
themselves capable (you, me, the everyman clown) can waggle
ass at terror.

What happened to us in a neonatal intensive care unit grew
into something fantastic. Not wonderful-fantastic, but mythical-
fantastic. Circus-fantastic. Before the NICU, there'd been nothing to overcome. I had never been hungry, sick, punched, or
abandoned. The sum total of my experience to that point had
been cold milk and warm cookies. My losses had been reason-
able, death only ever coming round to grandparents after many
long and loving years.

An uneventful life is a designation you can only appreciate in
hindsight.

In the middle of the night in my twenty-seventh week of
pregnancy, an ER team sprinted down a hallway pushing me
on a gurney. The wheels wobbled and squeaked as the doctors
shouted ahead, crashing through double doors, and the fluorescent lights on the ceiling blurred together like cards in spinning
bicycle spokes. Two babies were in my belly, and my belly had
failed. The doctors lifted them out of me, each son weighing two

pounds. A few hours later, in shock, I was wheeled into a room full of tubes, machines, and humans in peril.

INGLIS, BABY A. I saw an alien, purple and swollen, his legs splayed open, his body lifeless. A ventilator and medical tape blocked his face. I saw disaster.

INGLIS, BABY B. I saw a hairless kitten with legs the girth of his father's thumb. (Look at your thumb.) Pale skin hung off his bones as though it were two sizes too big. He was small—too small.

I saw lions and bears. I saw fire. I saw Liam and Ben.

. . . .

One of them died. I will explain.

. . . .

I could write a book about what happened and what came after, but instead I am watching *Beverly Hills Cop III* on Netflix. It is 3:00 a.m., years later. I am sitting in my empty house—empty for now—slouched down with my hair stuffed up under a woolly hat, a screen hot on my lap. I am covered in Norton Juster's Lethargians, the small gray creatures from *The Phantom Toll-booth*. They yawn and fawn, all of them a thick gray and gooey dough small enough to curl up by the dozens in earlobes and dangle from fingers and make everything so, so heavy.

The Lethargians found me, a new and delicious host, sometime in the empty space after my baby died, after everything fell apart. They've been here ever since, off and on, a slowly diminishing population. Eddie Murphy runs in high-waisted pants, his gun drawn. There's nothing the Lethargians love more than *Beverly Hills Cop III* on Netflix.

. . . .

Exquisite pain makes you hungry for transcendence, that first spirit high you chase in vain forevermore like a junkie. This is the great deception of heroin, they say. You will never again—may you hope to never again—get that close to the thin membrane between this world and whatever else is beyond it. If you chase it, you sink. Other bereaved people and allies say *We won't forget* and *You're doing great*, but maybe it's the not-forgetting that's landed me with Eddie Murphy at 3:00 a.m.

That's why it's hard to write a book. Experts write books. Enlightened people write books. You don't write a book during the fall, before you've got everything sorted. Only after. But I've been falling for years, scrambling up again, sorting out in fits and spurts, freshly sorted reasonings collapsing in on themselves to make space for new wrack. I worry any mandate of mine is fresh paint on rotten wood.

Fine. That's where all the power is, mine and yours. In shouting THIS SUCKS, totally unreconciled, and hearing another voice that's not just an echo of your own. If I squint, I can see a little wave from way over there. It's you. You're no less rattled than I am, but there you are, roasting squash and gutting sheds and yanking weeds to make space for things that might grow. I wave back.

. . . .

What happened was a crash C-section, two-pound twins born three months too soon by frantic incision and chest compressions. Heart surgery, brain surgery, morphine like a battleground. Two months later, we walked through sliding doors to fresh air and grass, away from antiseptic and toward a Cheerio-riddled floor. We were outside, finally, carrying one sibling brother and a baby boy (the one who survived), the second of two or three, depending on how you count.

. . . .

It was one of those Saturdays when the crowd on the waterfront bumps you around a bit. A blue sky, a warm breeze. Tall ships by the museum and ice cream cones.

It was our second day out of the hospital, his first day outdoors. At two months old, Ben weighed less than five pounds. Wrapped up against me, he wasn't much more than a mini football with half the air let out, the top of his head a long way from peeking out over the top of the mei tai. I shook like a leaf. What if he stopped breathing? What if I joggled him, bent him, lifted him wrong? What if something happened, something deep inside him that the alarms might have picked up? We were out and untethered without the usual assurance of twenty nurses.

A passerby stumbled, looking at me, at us, and elbowed her friend.

"That's not a real baby," she hissed, as they both gaped. "That's a doll. That woman is crazy!"

They disappeared through the crowd shaking their heads. I considered catching up, making them look. I wanted to tell them he had almost died, that his twin was gone. *I can hardly believe it either*, I wanted to say. I wanted to show her, shock her. I still do.

I didn't. The moment passed.

. . . .

In my dreams, the NICU room is dark and tidy with tight corners, like a theater stage after everyone has gone home.

They took out his ventilator, and I screamed at everyone to get out. It took twelve hours for Liam and I to let go of each other. Twelve hours and then I spoke aloud to nobody: *Please*. The air filled up with a < ? >, and I said *Please take care of my baby* and hands reached under and lifted him. The hands didn't belong to god. They felt older than that. They were gritty and thick with good clean muck, trailing seaweed, fluttering with moth wings.

I drive by the concrete box of the hospital from time to time. It makes me shudder. I wonder if I left anything behind: socks, skin cells, a ghost.

. . . .

The hole in me is patched up with cheesecloth, coagulated trauma, and German butter dumplings from *The Joy of Cooking*.

. . . .

Screw this story. I don't want this story. Why me, why us?
I throw it down and pick it up again. It's a battered thing but there it is, persistently, this story. I am bereaved. For the rest of my life I've got to drive around in this crashed car, this body, this disaster, and it's full of spilled blood and guts as much as the intact one—the Volkswagen people can see—is full of fossilized french fries and junk mail. This story grows new heads, multiplication plus subtraction followed by division. People walked a circle around it, looking at twisted metal with a hand on their chin.
People who look are better than people who don't.

. . . .

Days from his own death in 1847, Henry Lyte wrote what's arguably the most famous hymn ever put on paper:

> Swift to its close ebbs out life's little day
> Earth's joys grow dim; its glories pass away
> Change and decay in all around I see
> Friend who changest not, abide with me.

Friends who abide show up. They don't rush you through pain. They don't use guilt or shame, intentionally or otherwise. They don't try to fix or lecture. They don't start a single sentence with the words *at least . . . (you can try again / you already have a kid / you have your health*). Friends like that are a power higher than what you'll find in any holy place. Family can choose to be your friend like that. Friends can choose to be your family like that. They can be one in the same.

. . . .

This book is about you, not me. It reads like *I still can't drive past the hospital without holding my breath* or *Stick it, peanut gallery of faux-concerned onlookers, I never needed you.* But it's about your story through the lens of mine. When you share a pot of strong black tea with someone who has carried the same kind of loss, you affirm your intent to (1) pay attention to the rationalizations, instincts, or passing thoughts that feel like they belong and (2) reclaim power back from the bad luck and bullshit that keeps you feeling crippled. This book is a mirror. You, me—all of us—are going to be alright, someday, somehow. If you don't feel like that's possible in this moment, it's okay. Where you are right now is normal and rooted in the most ancient sort of love. You are not alone in it.

You might be here days after or years after. Either way, at one volume or another, some variation of the following has been, for a time, on continuous loop:

What the hell happened? Why? Why us?
What the hell, god?
How can I accept a completely unacceptable loss?
Why bother caring for myself when I couldn't care for my baby?
Why don't I ever want to be myself again?
Will I ever be myself again?
Will I always feel so alone? So cursed and forgotten and unheard and dismissed? So prickly and black humored and repeatedly collapsing? So stuck at the bottom of this well? What am I supposed to do with this life? My baby is gone. I am gone.

The answers:

I don't know.
[A cricket cricks.]
You can't. Until you do.
Because.
Because.
Sort of.
I'm going to put the kettle on.

Notes for the Everlost

CHAPTER ONE

The Immediate Protocol

A distant acquaintance called me the morning after
her baby was found not breathing. *I don't know anyone
else who's been through this,* she sobbed. *I don't know
how to live anymore.* This is what I said to her then,
and in our conversations since.

MATURITY TEACHES US to pause before offering opinion,
even if we think we'll be helpful. Especially then. Humility is in not telling other people what to do but in supporting others as they determine what they should do for themselves.

I'm not going to be humble right now. I have been to the same place, and I'd like to share with you some things I wish someone had shared with me. It might be helpful, if you're a short time from your loss.

1. *Don't apologize.*
It's foolish to the point of reckless to be sorry for stepping on a land mine. Stop it. Don't apologize for being sad. Don't apologize for reaching for the memory and substance of a baby who barely—or never—drew breath. Don't apologize for speaking to the dead. Don't apologize for no longer fitting into the ideal. Don't apologize for subjecting everyone who loves you to worry. They worry because they care. Don't apologize for making other people uncomfortable with the fact that you've just gotten the

lower half of your body blown off. *I'm sorry. I'm a bloody mess. I'm so sorry.*

Stop it.

2. Call upon your imagination to deal with dragons.

Honor all the snarling dogs, mouthless faces, and circling sharks that swarm in your head. They're trying to tell you something. Listen. They are your story trying to find its shape, and they all flail a bit when they're so new. Rilke said: "Perhaps all the dragons in our lives are princesses who are only waiting to see us act, just once, with beauty and courage. Perhaps everything that frightens us is, in its deepest essence, something helpless that wants our love."

Your dragons want you to remember how significant we all are, and how insignificant we all are. They are not against you. Consider them differently. They bring a heat that will become the core of some of the very best of you. Don't turn away. They're made of love. They reflect how badly we need to give and receive it. Imagination helps.

3. Forgive.

Some acquaintance in a grocery store lineup will say *I can relate. My dog died last year.*

A moment of big-eyeballed silence right now, seriously, for all the dead dogs.

Buff up your gallows humor. Share it with others who have had to endure the grocery store too. And the Thanksgiving tables, bridal showers, airport check-ins. Then forgive people for not knowing what to say, for filling the vacuum with every wrong thing. The quicker you realize most humans are artless thugs when faced with someone else's grief, the quicker you'll get over it when you meet one.

It's easy to forgive the random jerks. It's a lot harder to forgive friends and family who turned away from you. Or worse yet, who turned toward you to tell you to get over it, brushing your sadness off as a pregnancy gone awry. People may throw their own baggage and unresolved demons at you, trying to solve themselves by solving you. People may say *Stop making everyone uncomfortable.* They are uncomfortable because they are afraid. Forgive fear. Or at least, choose not to eat those rotten apples.

4. *Know you don't have to be whole to be normal.*
By the time you're an adult, you're rare if you have any less than three or four sizable chunks gnawed off your body, mind, or soul by one trauma or another. An apparently whole-looking person is not a wizard. They are a con man hiding behind a velvet curtain. Wholeness is something to prize only if you care most about the superficial. Let go of it and revel in plentiful company.

Every one of your emotions, outbursts, or lapses in social grace is 100 percent normal. In this extraordinary loss, you are ordinary. This is good. Your rage is normal. Your speechlessness is normal. Your running-off-at-the-mouth is normal. Your inability to know what you need is normal. Your difficulty occupying the same body that let you down—that's normal. Your falling out with faith—that's normal too.

A couple of years after my baby died, I pulled my car to the side of the road, suddenly struck with the sound of Liam gulping for breath. I was shaking so badly I couldn't drive. I leaned out the open door and almost threw up in a commuter parking lot. Years later my brain still hosts moving slideshows of Ben, Liam's surviving twin, dying in increasingly ridiculous ways. A hungry shark at Freda's Beach! A live grapeshot cannonball hidden in the grass at the old British garrison! A broken buckle, and he falls out of a roller coaster car! He is swallowed by a hippo. He is wearing safari beige and has a camera around his neck. He is crushed in the hippo's esophagus. I see his eyes close and his face go down. The hippo coughs up the camera and swims away. I scream at the hippo, begging him to eat me too. He disappears beneath the water.

You are not broken, and you are not failing. Neither am I.

5. Happiness can't be manufactured.
Harmony can. Parent yourself to protect it.

Imagine a child who is urgently upset, tired, hungry, sick, or injured. As a parent or caregiver, you would step in: *This needs to be taken care of and it needs to be taken care of now.* You'd act with empathy and immediacy, without shaming. You would address whatever lapse or shortfall was unaddressed. Food. Sleep. A Band-Aid. You'd make it better. Are you tantrumming with upset? Losing your mind with exhaustion? Afraid of the dark? Parent yourself.

Grief is most intolerable when there's a gap between what you need and what you're getting. The gap is the discord in which minds and relationships fester. The gap is created when you're too afraid—too committed to the illusion of wholeness—to say:

I need that day on my own.
I need to go back to that place.
I need help / antidepressants / therapy / a hot beach.
It's time to do something with those ashes.
Don't touch that urn.

Take a day off, a week off, a month. Give yourself friends or solitude, conversation or silence. Protect your needs whether it's three months out, six months, one year, or five. You have total agency over your well-being. Keep yourself away from poison. Give bullies a wide berth. Parent yourself: simply make sure you, a beloved child, have your needs met.

We don't judge a river for overflowing or slowing to a trickle.

We consider the conditions: pressure fronts, storms, drought, rain, wind. None of it is abnormal. It is the raucous, relentless, and sometimes unscrupulous nature of nature. It does what it must. But when people start messing with a river—trying to divert it, alter its flow, use it for other purposes, change its course—it becomes a disaster. Nature, when protected and cared for and allowed to be what it is, can be perfectly harmonious as long as we don't interfere with our agenda. So can grief.

Think of what you'd categorize as your worst moments: when you drank too much, overate, or self-medicated in a way you knew was not good for you. Think of when you said or did something you regretted or didn't sleep for a week or dropped the ball in your career or curled up in a dark room wanting nothing more than just that. In those moments we bristle at grief and hate ourselves for failing at it. It's a double-decker sandwich of misery. You are already dealing with empty arms, a flawed body, spiritual crises, relationship crises, identity distortions, sexual disconnects, survivor's guilt, and social isolation. This is the baseline after a baby dies. This is plenty. Don't add to it by being angry at yourself for not putting on a more palatable show.

There was never anything wrong with you. There still isn't. The next day dawns. Your worst is not who you are. You are not defined by your despair. Your worst was a tantrum, the most justified of all. Your parent—the parent of you, within you—loves you anyway, always, unconditionally.

· · · · · · · ·

Most human beings acquire the truth fragment by fragment, on a small scale, by successive developments, cellularly, like a laborious mosaic. There are very few who receive it, complete and staggering, by instant illumination.

—ANAÏS NIN, *The Diary of Anais Nin, vol. 3*

In the last moments, you looked at your baby and thought the same thing I did:

Please live. I don't mind if you dye your hair Kool-Aid blue. I don't mind if everything you believe turns out to be different from what I believe. I don't care who you love or how you love, as long as you find some and give some. I don't mind what you're into, as long as you're safe. I want to see the things that make you smile. I want you to have the chance to be. To be happy. Please live.

Then your baby died, like mine, and you received the most terrible and most effective lesson in unconditional love. You might have thought you knew what it was before, but you didn't. Not properly. Now you do.

CHAPTER TWO

As Much as I Can Remember

The Story of Liam and Ben

April 23, 2007. *Last night I dreamed my babies were born too soon. They were from another planet. They had acorns for knees and elastic legs and didn't cry. I stared at them and they stared at me with the giant, almond-shaped eyes widely reported by abductees. They knew everything there is to know. Then I woke up.*

THE TWIN BABIES of my pregnant dreams were science fiction, with fluorescent lights and scrubbing sinks. Days after the dream, after I woke up, shaken, and wrote it down, it unfolded just like that.

· · · · · · · · ·

The ultrasound technician had diagnosed me as having a particular form of twinning that carried a risk: "They're in two uterine sacs, which is good," she said. "But they share one placenta. We'll scan you weekly to make sure one baby doesn't start getting bigger than the other."

"What happens if that happens?" I asked.

"Oh, you don't have to worry about that."

"What's it called?"

"Twin-to-twin transfusion syndrome," she said.

In nonmedical terms, it's a gravity problem. The top baby drains and the bottom baby floods, with a pressure that overwhelms and damages major organs. But the phenomenon usually happens in increments over a series of months. For us, it was a torrent that went from perfect calm to its fatal worst inside of a couple of days. I hobbled around the backyard cradling my belly like a medicine ball, berating myself for not being able to handle a multiple pregnancy, convinced I couldn't possibly get any bigger. I paced. I tried to sleep and couldn't.

Be tougher than this. You still have three months to go.

I can't do this for three more months. I can't get any bigger. My stomach is going to explode.

It did. My placenta abrupted, sending me into labor at twenty-seven weeks. The medical resident frowned, listening, confirming only one heartbeat. Then the room turned upside-down. The sprint on the gurney. I was spun into place, strapped down. *Make a fist.* My belly, rock hard with catastrophic fluid, was set upon by a splash of antiseptic. A tube was shoved between my legs and rolling machines crashed into walls. *Get the neonatal team in here, stat!* A mask fell over my face, another urgent voice in my ear. *Four deep breaths, give us four deep breaths, then you'll feel cold . . .* then it all went black. Then blinding light again, immediately, it seemed. I wondered if there had been some mistake. All sound in the operating room was muffled, like being underwater. I couldn't speak and couldn't see my babies. While I had been out, the doctor had peeled off my skin like a sausage casing from scalp to toes. He must have. He said *Nurse, blow torch* and fire-carved black swirls all over my insides like thousand-year petrogylphs. Woman-giver; thunder; smashed nest; broken birds. Then he put me back together, but from the moment I opened my eyes again I could feel grit and scar tissue under my skin. Ten years later, I still can.

A few hours after it happened, a neonatologist sat at my bedside.

One is stable. Blood transfusions
But the other
Kidneys, lungs, heart
Brain severely compromised
Fourth-degree bilateral bleed
Coma-like state
Do not resuscitate
Sign this
Kate
Kate
She is not hearing me
Can somebody please call the nurse
Kate
Get her into a wheelchair
It's the morphine
Kate

. . . .

Through the halls of the NICU my wheelchair passed machines that fed bloodstreams, pumped hearts, and filled lungs. Tangles of tubes and wires encased plastic boxes swarming with masked people in paper slippers. They wheeled me in between two incubators.

They are out
They are out
I am empty
They should not be out
They are out

I approached them as I would a live bomb.

Oh my god
Oh god no
I'm so sorry

It felt like a decision. I couldn't help it.

I hate you, body. I will hate you forever.

. . . .

". . . Severe cerebral palsy. And he's unlikely to ever see or walk, and there will be seizures and lifelong diapers and repeated surgeries."

The doctor gestured to what must be apparent, like clouds indicative of storm, and I blinked stupidly.

"See these patches of white?" he dragged his finger over the screen. "That's damaged tissue, if there's anything there at all. There's not much functional brain left."

I slumped in the chair. He continued.

"But he's here, isn't he? He can hiccup, and he is breathing on his own, and while some of that is reflex, the fact that he can swallow is a miracle."

He nodded neatly and backed out of the room.

I hate you, body. I will hate you forever.

. . . .

A few days later, we were alone, on the night shift. I trespassed through his porthole. The tape that held the ventilator to his head had come unstuck on a lock of downy brown, the ragged edge curling up.

I love you. I will love you forever.

There was condensation inside the tube, the lung outside his body. As it pushed oxygen in and out, tiny bubbles wiggled and burst.

"Say something," the nurses would tell me. "Let him hear you."

It's a horrible thing, isn't it, that shame was in the way. But it was. I was struck dumb with it. I didn't know what to do other than to cry and say *love love love* and *sorry sorry sorry*. That night, I tried, a disconnected babble that turned into a wish.

Lili love, the ocean swells and makes thunder, and it's filled with treasure and ghosts all churned up and dashed and smashed wood and bits of twine and all kinds of lost and abandoned things, and when the sun comes out, the ocean turns into diamonds and the wind makes it sing. I want you to see it. I want you to see it so much.

· · · · · · · ·

Ben was two pounds of spitfire. Barely a week after his birth he pantomimed outrage as if to say *Leave me alone. Go away. I don't wanna. I mad. I so mad.* I scrubbed in, pressed my ear against the porthole inches from his thrashing face, and there it was. Not a cry, but an open mouth and an angry, tiny mewing.

Get mad, kid. Mad makes heat. Heat is good.

Liam never cried. He peered bewildered through slivers of black.

· · · · · · · ·

To live at the hospital was to live inside a hive of bees. Pumping milk in the middle of the night, the wall shook at my back. It was a living place, a dying place, with ducts and fans and machines with accordion throats that groaned and heaved, mechanical innards inhaling and exhaling. A single, long alarm would ring across the paging system: NEONATAL TEAM TO ROOM 311, STAT. NEONATAL TEAM TO ROOM 311, STAT. NEONATAL TEAM TO ROOM 311, STAT. Said once I could pretend not to hear, drift back into uneasy sleep. But echoing three times in my own private darkness, I was boggle-eyed.

They said that for us, once. Ten minutes later a familiar thrum would approach in the skies, growing louder. The helicopter would land on the roof above my head, deafening then slowing, and I'd imagine the running footsteps and stretcher wheels and shouting. We were buried in countless layers of distress like the smallest of solid centers in a Russian nesting doll. Parents kept their eyes on their own incubators, thrown together to unwillingly witness one another's heartbreak.

You resort to almost constant prayer in there no matter what you believe, even if it's on the far end of the spectrum of crossing fingers, throwing salt over a shoulder, or knocking on wood. The humanity of it all is too thick to ignore. The air is both stale and stirred up, pulsing electric like the blades of the medevac.

. . . .

I undressed and put on a johnny shirt backward so it opened at the front. Then I scrubbed in up to my elbows; sat in a recliner on wheels; watched as a team of nurses opened the incubators, navigating through a network of tubes and wires to lift the babies up, various interventions draping alongside from their two-pound bodies to the machines; heard them calling for one thing to be detached, then reattached—*turn this way, move that cart*—lay still as they placed one on my skin, then the other; made a nest with my arms; pushed back as someone reclined us; held my breath as they reconnected the machines; shifted myself this way and that as a nurse wrapped the three of us in a warm flannel swaddle; sighed as they pulled the curtain and left.

I looked down at my babies, faces squashed against me, mouths flopped open.

It's hard to be alive and mad, isn't it, mama. Shush, mama.

All three of us got damp and sweaty as tired parents and babies do. All three of us stopped fussing. Two hours passed in a blink. I opened my eyes and the nurses were waiting there, needing to do their rounds.

"You slept," one of them said approvingly. "You slept the whole time. You all did."

"He squeezed my finger," I replied, groggy. Doubt rang through my head like a taunt. *That's only a reflex.*

"Of course he did! He loves his mommy," she smiled evenly, perhaps a little rehearsed, a little too pert, doing her best, I imagine, as she swept in to remove them back to their wombs.

. . . .

"Whatever you do, know this," the pediatric palliative care doctor whispered. "This is not your decision. The brain surgery was too much, the hydrocephalus on top of the bleed. He is failing on life support, so we will orchestrate his passing to be in your arms. Otherwise, he will die when you're not here. This is not your decision. This is all of us paying attention to him."

He was kind. We signed the piece of paper.

"Terminal babies with uncompromised brains come off a ventilator and pass away in minutes," he spoke slowly. "For Liam, it could take a couple of hours because he's jumbled. But he needs us to try and let him go."

I nodded, numb. Machines were switched off, wires detached, tubes removed until he was just a boy. He lay on my bare chest and for the first time, at six weeks old, I saw and felt his face and his body without anything attached to it. The nurses loitered, clearing the debris of his intervention, and I shrieked GET OUT and they did.

. . . .

I'm sorry.
  I'm so sorry.

. . . .

I will find you, love.

I will magic myself into milk for you when I die. I will be thirty-four again and I will wrap you up snug to me and I will know all your dimples and moles and scents, forever and ever, and that will be my afterlife, to walk with you.

. . . .

Lili, I'm sorry.

. . . .

For the twelfth time in as many hours the resident listened intently, her stethoscope at his back. He hadn't taken a single breath in several minutes. He had grown cold, an inside-out draining. She declared him, again, to be faint but lingering. "His lungs are no longer working, but his brain doesn't seem able to tell his heart to stop."

She left the room. I shifted, and he shuddered and gulped and rasped, a drowning victim breaking the surface. His father and I cried. It was like that all night.

Just after dawn, during another one of these spells of breathless stillness, a construction crew pulled into the parking lot below. Their thumping shadows passed our window through the curtain, up the scaffolding with bagged lunches and coils of wire. We had taken away Liam's ventilator at the previous day's dusk. The next day was beginning.

Please

I could not release my baby into nothingness. I needed his end to be more than the rearrangement of dust. I spoke aloud. I don't know why.

Please

The room filled up. Something arrived, listening.

Please take care of my baby

At that exact moment, I felt hands reach softly underneath him and his weight was lifted from my chest. I felt intense peace, joy, and lightness, a reunion, like the tickly thrill of throwing yourself into the arms of a long-away loved one at an airport baggage hall. None of those feelings were mine. I was an observer. The presence in the room took him. It had been waiting to. Then the air cleared.

The shell of my son rested on my skin as it had for the past twelve hours. There was no rattle, no heave, no murmur. Nothing confirmed it except the intense feeling of some kind of loving sorcery. I called for the resident again. She listened with the stethoscope. This time she exhaled and nodded.

"He's gone."

It is not in my nature to pray. The idea of an interventionist god has always been offensive to me, and religious morality (and the exclusion and war that comes along with it) even more so. In a state of pure exhaustion and despair, I had drifted toward a spirit realm only as I begged for more morphine for him—just in case.

Please, please, please let there be some meaning, some help, anything

The first time in my life I spoke aloud to nature, the only god my imagination finds palatable, I gave her permission to take my son.

There are 43,200 seconds in twelve hours. Liam died that second.

· · · · · · · ·

I don't get it, a friend wrote once. *Not only do I not "get it"—it pisses me off when people say there's a god. People who would put more stock in some imagined higher power than in real people and treat that imagined being with more respect than they treat real people. If god's so great, why did the Rwandan genocide happen? Why does random tragedy strike good and honest people? Why do people who sincerely think they're good and honest do terrible and selfish things, still carrying on thinking they're good and honest because they wave a bible around?*

(Friend: one. The gods: zero.)

Bullshit, she continued. *There's no heaven and no hell. There is only now. As I age, I grow more sure of this, that my life will end when my body expires, that I will live only in memory, that I might support a tree or a berry bush when I'm gone. I find comfort in the continuity of my atoms.*

I would only, if ever, subscribe to a god who would fully endorse disbelief and questioning, recognizing we were explicitly programmed for it. Fossils and old-growth forests and the fascinatingly irrefutable age of our planet's rocks negate any literal interpretation of the holy books, though they've all got poetry and gravitas. The problem is that religious organization of any bent corrupts itself into a parade of bullies and sheep, sustaining itself by making critical thinking the bad guy.

I'd like to think there's something out there, though. Something older. A spark. A flame. Millions of them reflected millions upon millions of times as we observe the energy and wondrous interplay of the natural world.

So I replied *Don't you think there's too much mystery to reduce it all to dust?*

Nope, she wrote.

I tried to explain. *The morning Liam died, something was in the room with us. I could almost touch it. It's left me open to the possibility of a presence that's a lot more complex and sensible and sad and more uncertain and more full of love than any religion would ever allow.*

And she replied, *Not to dishonor that night for you, but don't you think that was just your heart?*

Nope, I wrote, but not without a pause.

I have wondered if I was unhinged, if I invented magic where none existed. I've wondered if the presence in the room that day was just the intensity of the moment. Perhaps he was just an egg and a sperm that divided and gestated into one of two human babies, and who was betrayed by his mother's placenta, was born sick, and then died to be turned to ash and set loose on a lake because his parents are sentimental, thinking it would somehow make him free to come and go as he pleased. He did not watch our red canoe. He did not come to me in that special kind of light. He was not brave. His brain was simply so damaged that he was numb to the ophthalmologist who propped his eyelids open with wire spiders to prod his retinas while Ben screamed throughout the same procedure, as healthy babies do. He was not my resolute protector. He was just a baby we called Liam because that's what popped into my head at finding out we'd need two names instead of one. Perhaps.

Contemplating dust and the randomness of atoms doesn't rob me, or him, of any grace. It is grace. Its energy granted me the most shocking moment of my life—a moment I don't think I manufactured. But of course I wouldn't think that, would I? For a long time, the question lingered like a stink. Was I grasping at straws? Had that moment been the impulse of my own desperation? Had Liam simply disappeared into nothing?

I had to smile with my eyes as well as my mouth or else my living children would see. I decided to hang on to the gift I'd been given: to that very firmly felt, wholly unexpected lifting. The presence. I decided to stop studying it. When his struggle ended and his life left his body, something took him for me. I felt it. There was palpable peace, joy, and lightness. It wasn't mine.

· · · · · · · ·

The mountain forests of British Columbia are the world's most grand cathedrals. Hallways and altars and grand columns thousands of years old rise from rich, deep moss-velvet. We returned home to Nova Scotia, land of pirates and rumrunners and a meat grinder sea, to have babies near family and buy an old house with some land for cheap. For a long time, with no peaks, the horizon felt empty. The woods were a shag carpet of stunted and unassuming gnarliness. Legions of black spruce stood like matchsticks in comparison to the West, more determined than glorious.

The day Liam died, we drove home for a rest after the night-long vigil of his death, leaving his surviving twin in the nursery and longing for the sticky and oblivious toddling of their older brother. I rested my head against the car window and stared out at the blur of brackish Eastern forest. I had told him, as we lay through spells of breathing and spells of not: *Climb in through my ear and sit down cross-legged behind my eyes. I'll move my head back and forth and show you things.*

He had died that morning but the world still existed. Cars on the highway. People waiting in drive-throughs for double-doubles and Boston cream doughnuts. As we crossed into Lunenburg County, I saw a bog of threadbare jack pines. *Look, Lili. Look how they're proud of their prickly tuft. They get up to mischief with the crows.*

They were no cathedral, but with eyes for him, they were suddenly just as grand. For the year that followed he was inside me again, with all his voices that might have been. He sassed, a teenager. He sat for tea with me, a father. On darker days I snarled at myself that none of it was real. I don't know it matters either way. We talked, and he stayed. That's how it felt until the window closed.

Lili baby. You would have loved all this.

. . . .

I peered over the edge of the canoe and saw flecks of bone and ash swirling on the brandy-brown lake like stars in an upside-down sky. *How did I get here, watching the remains of my son drift in an eddy?*

Trees and clouds and blades of grass throbbed with the same presence that had brushed up thick and vivid against my cheek as he died, but they said nothing. Later, in the cabin, I sat as close as I could to the fire, staring at embers until my face flushed hot.

Fuck you, death.

Thank you, death.

Death smiled in a tired sort of way. It always does.

· · · · · · · ·

People saw us and lurched. Some turned away. Some asked, staring at their shoes, how we were doing. I learned how to respond with a nonresponse.

It's been rough, but we're okay.

The more we find out about just how injured he was, the more we realize he couldn't stay.

We're just trying to focus on what we have.

I had spent Liam's life wandering hospital hallways and nursing stations and pumping rooms with rat's nest hair, red eyed and puffy faced. Those six weeks brought more tears, terror, and panic than I'd ever felt in my life. Then he was gone, and sometimes in conversation I'd slip into the clinical highlight reel because I couldn't handle one more *We're okay* for the sake of keeping the room comfortable. I'd either make people cry or stare at their shoes. I'd like to think I didn't mean to, but maybe I did.

Alone, I'd smell antiseptic. I'd hear the machinery, the alarms, the chilling squirt of the line into his scalp. I'd feel his skin on mine. For years, I would meet people and think: *Ask me how many children I have. Ask me so I can tell you three, but only two. Ask me what happened.*

What I wanted was a lapel pin: I HAVE AN INVISIBLE SON. And more rooms that didn't mind. I wanted people with the fortitude to hear his name. And when I found rooms and people like that, I didn't need to say much after all.

. . . .

As she took Liam's body away, our nurse had pressed a ceramic heart on a string into my hand. It had a hole in the middle of it. *He will have the other piece*, she whispered, as she wrapped his body in a blanket, carrying him as though he were still alive. *You will always be connected.*

She left the room with the bundle that was him. I wouldn't see his body again. The next time I held him, he was inside an urn. I didn't know. I don't know what I thought, but I didn't know. Why didn't I follow her down the hall? How could I have done that? I passed him to her the way you pass a baby around a dinner table, like I needed a break to fill my plate.

Take it easy, Mom. His fifteen-year-old voice. *You were tired. They had to do it and so did you.*

I wore the ceramic heart around my neck until I caught it kissing someone else under the high school bleachers. At my friend Bon's house, months later, I peered closer and startled when something caught my eye in a photo of her son Finn's urn. Around the neck of it rested a little heart. It was the center of the empty one given to her the night he died. It matched mine.

I had been cycled through the steps the hospital takes when a mother loses a baby.

Did the fact that it had been procedure make it any less genuine or meaningful? Instinctually, in that moment: yes. I had been deeply moved. I had hung on to it sometimes, feeling the smooth warmth of it against my breastbone where his head had been. In some boardroom, a committee had decided a ceramic hole-in-heart would be line item number twelve on the Infant Mortality Response Strategy. I had fallen for it, a bureaucratic trinket.

Suddenly I wanted to take it off. The empty heart didn't connect me to him at all.

This was just a contrivance. But how will I have Liam with me, if it's not this? Dammit, I just gave him to her and she took him away, and I didn't know that would be it, and that was it.

He was gone all over again. My stomach turned. I was desperate for something to hold, but I didn't want it to be from the lobby gift shop of the building where he died. I put the ceramic heart into the sailmaker's chest where I keep all his things: a three-inch-wide diaper from the NICU stack, oxygen leads, the blue tape that held it all in place, the daily journals the nurses wrote to us. I never wore the heart again, but I've forgiven it. It means something different now. The empty heart was never a match for Liam's. It was a match to other mothers and fathers who fell into this pit, stayed there a while, and eventually climbed out.

· · · · · · · ·

Two months after he died, on the eve of our release, I sat in the transition nursery feeding Ben. A young nurse sat in a rocking chair next to me, resting for a moment. After a long span of quiet, she made a confession.

"I was there, you know, when they were born."

Her name was Julie. I had been walking around with staples in my belly, and she'd been there when it happened. On the night everything went wrong, she'd seen my guts all sprawled out. I hadn't known. She continued, almost in a whisper.

"It was the scariest thing I've ever seen."

Thinking they were pulling up bootstraps, some people would say the most awful things. They'd say *Count your blessings* or *Everybody hurts* or *You're not the only one that's gone through pain.*

It was cruel, maddeningly so. I wasn't pornographically sad. I was a mixed bag of dark days and decent days. I tended to regular things, hiding what spun nonstop behind my eyes. In flashes of misguided vulnerability with the wrong person I'd share a small piece of the sadness and they'd say *Why do you think you are so special?* I'd stare slack-jawed, in shock.

In a parallel universe, I stood up for myself: *You are the one who isn't brave. I am the giant.*

Every now and then, a different sort of person—someone who wasn't afraid—would look right at me and say *I am so upset this happened to you.* I would crouch over it hungrily like a bear with a carcass. It was sustenance.

It was the scariest thing I've ever seen, said Julie, who had been with us all along.

"Thank you," I said, which is as much a strange thing to say as it is the only thing.

Years later, Julie landed in the NICU with her own twins, one of whom died. It was almost poetically eerie, as tragic coincidences go. She wrote to me *How did you get through this?*

I don't know, I responded. *But you will.*

. . . .

I had always assumed a certain life order: childhood, school, puberty, sex, career, taxes, marriage, gestation, birth, motherhood, gestation, birth, sweatpants, early morning hockey rinks, drugstore highlights, an empty nest, grandmotherhood, retirement, twilight, illness, death. I assumed nothing less for the ones I would love.

For my son it was injury, death, birth, injury, cutting, a rally, more cutting, then twilight, then death again, all inside six weeks of climate-controlled antiseptic beige. Now, he is decade-gone particles of blood and bone and muscle burned up and scattered in a lake and churned a thousand times over in the bellies of a perfect and peaceful ecosystem. He is my darling but he doesn't need me, and that's not motherhood. It's something else.

As we age we collect spirit darlings. They rub together to form the heat of lost opportunity, unrequited adoration, hope, fear, tragedy. At first this heat sears and spits. Especially the first few times. It will happen again, and again, and each time we will absorb the lesson a fraction more until we learn it fully on our own deathbed: love is the only thing. There is no riddle, and there is no unfairness. All we can do is feel love and offer it without requiring it in return.

That is what this is.

. . . .

I am dreaming. Liam died. I am driving to the hospital to see Ben.

Something took him, didn't it? Or was it just me?

The world splits in two. In one, the front end of my car is crushed, splattered in blood and fur. In the other I swerve, and the deer escapes, and so do I.

CHAPTER THREE

What Now

Finding your way through grief after the first year, when you
begin the work of integrating (a better word than *healing*).

Y OU'VE GOT to get up and make breakfast.
You'll lie there for a while resisting, thinking all kinds of
insensible things people think when they get up to make breakfast after somebody dies. Especially after a child dies. Like how
you don't deserve to eat. Like how your jerk body just carries on,
dumb and deaf and pumping like the meat suit it is, taking stuff
in and processing it and making energy and pushing it out. Why
does one soft machine work when another doesn't? It'll make
you stare at a bag of bagels, sighing, for longer than you should.

A few words about sighing. This is important.

If crying is the body-wracking shrieks of a three-year-old separated from a bookstore train set, I didn't cry every day. If crying
is a face dripping silently while staring into space for a minute
or an hour, then maybe it was every day, and for quite some
time. This is how the bereaved follow their love. All other ways
are closed. And as soon as we ease away from the sighing and
crying and staring into space—who knows when—we'll mourn
the mourning.

In trauma, the concrete that separates regular life from golden
tickets and glass elevators and giant peaches thins to a veil.
Through it, we can see and hear and sense the other side. When
you cling to it, you're not wallowing. You are integrating.

Grief is not an illness, a diagnosis, or a constant state. Grief is the bruise after a blow. Blackening is normal. Swelling is normal. Then a rotten sort of putrid. Then it sinks beneath the skin, failing to mark you anymore, failing to excuse you, returning you to the masses before you're ready. You'll miss the black and blue because as soon as it fades, you go from "honoring" to—as your onlookers might say—"dwelling," that damnable word.

The losses that can follow loss—those of identity, personality, spark, ambition, humor, sex, focus, optimism, appetite, intimacy, faith, partnership, friendship, self-love, unconditional acceptance—feel irrevocable. If only we could lighten ourselves of the burden of counting what's fair and what's not. But we can't. It's the great cosmic prank: our inability to stop counting is the very missing link between us and our simian cousins. All the gods know it.

· · · · · · · ·

The pamphlet was a piece of paper folded twice, a photocopy of a photocopy. On the front was a line drawing of a woman in bell bottoms and a turtleneck sweater, her head in her hands. The title read, *Booklet of Normal Feelings.*

At one of the hospital's fruit-punch-and-cheese support groups for parents in the NICU, a social worker had appraised my glassy eyes. Reaching for the melon balls with one hand, she pushed the pamphlet across the table with the other.

"You should read this."

I looked at it with a frozen face as the parents around me chatted nervously about jaundice and reflux. The room hung there, a study of two-bite muffins and Styrofoam cups. I stumbled out into the hall and she followed me.

"You forgot your bag." She pressed it into my arms. "Kate, I think we should talk about what you might need, you know, to get through this."

"Okay," I replied. She gave me a ten-dollar gas coupon. Then she walked away.

They provide the diagnostics, the pharmaceutical goo, the doctors trained in medical science as well as the compassionate art of saying *We just have no way of knowing.* That's a big mandate. Often too big to tend to the emotional shrapnel for families as well. The hospital must triage, assigning degrees of urgency, and my feelings as the parent of a gravely injured or dying child are way down the list. Even if they weren't, how might we better initiate new arrivals to this alien world? Is it even possible to mitigate the shock of it? How might we better protect and honor parents in the face of do-not-resuscitate orders for their baby?

We, the suffering and the bereaved, can't possibly be cut loose in a world where people still run for the bus like it matters. We can't possibly.

But we are.

. . . .

DISCHARGED: cleared; dismissed; freed; fulfilled; detonated.

. . . .

Pictures showed what I couldn't see in front of me when it was happening. He bloomed as he graduated from the ventilator, almost plump in his stability. But a few days later, his head began to swell. On top of the flood in my womb, oxygen deprivation at birth, brain surgery, and heart surgery, he had developed hydrocephalus—water on the brain.

Two weeks later, poring through the images, I could see with the same brutal clarity what the nurses must have seen. His face was a grimace. The shape of his head, the pallor of his skin . . . he was lost. Even as they wheeled him away for the surgery that hoped to save what was left of his brain, I hadn't considered the possibility he would take a turn. I was placated by the fact that he looked so much better than he had at birth. I dared to hope he may not only survive but be unscathed. Almost like a healthy baby.

Delusion can be self-protection. We walk beside our children and hold their hands as long as we're able, even when we despair at their path. Especially then.

. . . .

You might worry your heart is full of holes and that a heart full of holes can't function properly. Now think of all the things that do exactly what they are meant to do thanks to their holes, large or microscopic: sponges, soufflés, the foam inside life jackets. Your holes are buoyant. So are mine. Your holes make you lighter than you look.

. . . .

In the odd space between Liam's death and Ben's release, I sat one night at home, pumping breast milk for the next day's hospital shift as Evan's two-year-old voice echoed in the gurgling empty of his bath.

"I show mama!" He careened around the corner. "MAMA!"

He leaped into my lap and threw his pudgy arms around my neck, steaming-fresh. "I ha' BUSY DAY! I see FWIENDS. I pway in a-pwaygwound, a-big TWAINS! A-dis way, mama. I a-jammies. Cuddle, pweeze!"

"I can't love. Soon! Mama has to make baby food."

Evan curled up and watched, his eyes fixed on the drip-drip- drip.

"Mama make a-boobie milk," he declared. "Aah . . . [as if deciding] a-dis one for Ben, a-dis one for Leee-am."

I decided it may as well be then.

"Evan love, Liam doesn't need mama's milk anymore. He's a

star now, watching over you. He's okay, he's a happy baby now. But he won't be with us."

He scrunched his forehead.

"No mama. Dis one's for Leee-am. Dat one's for Ben. Dis one's for Leee-am. Leee-am! Thomas. James. Skarloey."

He huffed off importantly to arrange his trains into parking lots. From the other room came a *crash-bang* as a basket was overturned.

"Aah! Misser Toppem Hat. Liam. Twubblesome twucks. GORDON!"

Gravity is randomly selective. The bare bum and wet neck of a warm two-year-old can fend off the pull for a time. Lots of other things can too. A cast iron skillet full of tomatoey French lentils simmered with marsala wine, the stirring of which gives you a twenty-four-minute reprieve from actively remembering your baby is gone. For a moment, things will be okay. You've made some nice supper. Gravity ambles off elsewhere to affect the mass of someone else.

. . . .

People at a loss for words might say stuff like this to you: *Your story makes me realize how easy we've got it / how insignificant my problems are / how lucky I am. I think my life is so hard but then I think of you.*

You'll imagine taking them by the shoulders, pulling them close, and kneeing them in the groin. Wait. No. A falling anvil! A flaming bag of dog shit! A trip wire and down they go, and you have a SLOW-MOTION REPLAY button and you hit it again and again.

They'll say *Thank you for reminding me to hug all my favorite people a little tighter today, because I can!*

You'll say *You're welcome.*

You'll stew about it for a few days. Then you'll soften up and let it go because you'll realize you might have once been, at best, at a loss for words. Or at worst, the justified recipient of someone else's fantasy flaming bag of dog shit. We are a clumsy bunch when it comes to tragedy, especially in the West. We don't understand it at all until we understand it too much.

Before Liam, I didn't know how perilous and unlikely it was to be alive. I knew it, but I didn't. His death was a total breakdown of every assumption I didn't know I'd been assuming. *What is good? What is love? Why everything?* I had felt intentional in my life to that point, but I'd been bumbling along eating crackers, futzing over the way my belly stuck out. The conundrums we inherit as sentient creatures . . . I thought I knew. But I didn't. Not to say you are unenlightened until you suffer deep pain. But that's how it was for me.

As the only animals who know we will die, how should we live? This is the sweet and futile agony. It's where every inner monologue comes from. We obsess over happiness, completeness, and chemicals that gently cover gray hair. We buy heart-shaped rocks painted with *Stand in Your Truth* and *Brave Is Free*. Somehow, despite knowing loss will happen to us—and that our own ashes will someday be inside an urn on the lap of somebody who loved us—it's still incomprehensible.

Yet here we are. Still bumbling, but awake. Hello, you.

In a dream you and I are wandering the streets. We've got black scarves over our faces and fistfuls of heart-shaped rocks. We are hunting for unbroken glass.

. . . .

After the first year, I would go for the odd stretch of days—sometimes even a week—without thinking of Liam. Not consciously, anyway. Then at the end of April I'd be scrambling an egg and my brain would jump out of its chair and shout IT'S ALMOST MAY, and I'd remember.

This time last year / two years ago / three years ago
He was still alive.
But it was all about to go wrong.

I'd remember my stretched-to-bursting roundness and the gurney. I'd remember Liam spread-eagled helplessly, purple and swollen, Ben so tiny that a photograph needed visual context like the grip of a fishing rod next to a trout at the bottom of a boat.

In that first year I spent a lot of time with my face squashed up against Ben's, spitty cheek to mouth, mouth to ear, whispering and tickling, pressing up against his skin with mine because it soothed him. Or maybe I needed a little for myself.

Nine years later, I shouted, "Kids, come quick! We're doing the cake rocket!"

It was Ben's birthday. There was a thunderous scramble as a dozen sets of feet came hurtling into the dining room to land in skids on the floor, all of them watching the waiting match, their mouths hanging open in smiles or chattering to each other:

Move over, you're sitting on my foot!
I saw one of these cake rockets once at my cousin's house!
What!? Fireworks! Did you get that at the Dollarama?
After this I am gonna get you!
Ha, ha no way!
Why are you only wearing one sock?
I wish Liam were here!

I heard Ben's voice as *pssshhh* the cake lit up.

Later that night, watching him with a puzzle: "Ben, that was nice today, by the cake, when you wished Liam were here."

"What?"

"When you said you wished Liam were here."

"I didn't say that out loud. Did I?"

"You did, love. It was nice."

He smiles distantly. He's unbothered and cheerful and busy. I think about all the brothers and sisters, aunts and uncles and grandparents, and you and me, reaching, laboriously and privately, to find our way. Calling on today's imagination to underpin tomorrow's integrated world, months or years later, in which we remember, pause, wish, and then run outside to shoot our best friend in the butt with a nerf gun.

. . . .

I still can't believe she's not alive anymore, wrote a friend of her baby girl. *That she was born so sick. That she lived for two months and then died. When does that stop happening, the disbelief?*

I replied, *Probably never. But it changes.*

First, the child—or the potential of the child—is gone. Then you feel gone, too. You spit venom at anyone who would dare presume to either cross this gulf or heckle you from the other side of it. Death has draped one and then two silky-thin veils over you: one is anger, and the other is concentrated affinity, compassion, and longing. The resulting effect is disordered, unconvincing either way.

A thousand and then a million things will call you into the world again, even if it's fleeting. Proper Scottish oatcakes steaming fresh on a cooling rack. Street art on your way home. A boss who says *Hey, you were great in there.* Even children—those belonging to other people or to you—will tap hairline fractures in your rage. But it's not the rage you have to learn to live with. It's the way you'll become ordinary again. It's how you'll become alright almost against your will. People will see you at a farmers market and whisper *Look, her baby died but there she is with a basket of Swiss chard. Gosh. The poor thing.* You'll see it on their faces and you'll feel a rush of betrayal, because you'd only been thinking *Yay! I got the last Swiss chard.* You weren't thinking of yourself as a poor thing. You might have not been thinking at all. Which might be a miracle. A horrible, normal, awful, blessed, guilt-ridden miracle.

On hearing the stories of other losses and illnesses and tragedies —some unfolding right now—I've found myself thinking *I could not survive that.* But I would, and you would. With bruises, with subsequent domino effects, with dreams of falling anvils and flaming bags of dog shit, with unexpectedly peaceful days or weeks that happen despite us; and then the tears come back and the wheel turns and turns. There is another side, sort of. We build a bridge. Every tear is a nail and every sigh is a hammer.

Don't go, my love. Don't go, my grief. Stay a little longer.

· · · · · · · ·

"I just forgot. I keep them in my makeup kit, and there were three slobby days in a row so I'd blown that month. Then when it came time to start another month I . . . forgot."

I was staring at the floor.

"Do you know what this is?" asked my doctor. She answered for me. "Subconscious self-sabotage. Please do not do this."

She pressed a refill prescription for birth control into my hand.

"I have more pills at home. Probably." I mumbled.

"I'm giving you this to make doubly sure," she replied. "I am sending you to the pharmacy with a police escort and porcupine-quill panties and a sandwich board hung around your neck that reads DO NOT IMPREGNATE ME: I AM EMOTION-ALLY UNSTABLE."

Something like that, amounting to *This is not the time. Not physically and not otherwise.* I denied I'd even consider it, but I was lying. I felt urgently in need of punishment, and pregnancy would be that. Punishment, penance, a screw you to the universe. Ten years later, I remember the soft, immediately post-trauma *Nope, nope, nope* of my doctor as the loving shush it was intended to be. And it applies to everything. Open space comes back again. But not until a bagel is just a bagel.

· · · · · · · ·

For a while, I drove a minivan. Then one of three assumed children died and all I could see in the rearview mirror was an unnecessary void. With the third row permanently folded down, the back was a cube van. Runaway cans of chickpeas and spare diapers and half-eaten, fossilized snack remnants rolled from port to starboard like rats on a battleship. So we sold it. As we drove away from the dealership in a secondhand Volkswagen, I turned around in my seat to keep the offending Mazda in sight as long as I could. I don't know why. I hated that thing.

Except I do know why. I had started to embrace the inevitable spectacle of three kids, of twins. Two highchairs, two hats, two Jolly Jumpers side-by-side. And a minivan. After the NICU, we emptied our house of extras and with every trip to the second-hand shop, I'd think *He never felt grass* and *He never heard music* and *He never tasted ice cream.* I watched through the rearview mirror with tears dripping off my chin. I wanted to need that van. From a new back seat Ben farted in his sleep, one of those rich, healthy toots, and the spell was broken.

· · · · · · · ·

A wise friend wrote to me: *Some think by expressing sadness or rage or self-pity, you are lacking in compassion by not remembering the suffering of others, or by making others uncomfortable. But by refusing grieving people the opportunity to pass through those dark emotions, we deny compassion to you.*

For a while, you may consciously or unconsciously deprive, self-medicate, self-isolate, or punish yourself. You may run away in small ways, or in big ones. There may be a jealousy of others you perceive to have been spared, and the guilt of feeling like you're wishing ill upon others (you're not). You're likely to have little patience for women whose labor complaints amount to pissing a little each time they sneeze. You certainly won't have patience for family members who make it broadly known you should get over it already. You may flee from pregnant women in supermarkets, one piece of hundreds in an instinctual jigsaw puzzle that also includes an intolerance for emotional chicken-shits, public panic attacks with no apparent trigger, and lead-balloon cremation jokes at neighborhood potlucks. It's necessary and normal, all of it. Hammers and nails.

The anarchist in me says SCREW GRACE. The anarchist in me wants that bumper sticker. The anarchist in me, remembering how grief felt in its early years, feels ferocious in defense of you in your early years. To install as a shield onto the surface of your brain and heart, because we all carry enough pain without volunteering for more:

Be an unnavigable hermit as long as you need to be. Acknowledging the pain is the only way to allow it to get on with its business, to scab over. Anyone who tells you you're doing it wrong can eat shit for breakfast.

Grief is necessary, honorable, and healthy. Ordinary will find you again when you're ready. The people around you will either adapt and earn their stripes or they won't.

Grief is neither finite nor linear, but there is another side to it. You are already a bigger, more open, more powerful person than anyone who's currently making you feel small. Despite not being reliably even-keeled, you are more compassionate now than you were before. You know how it feels to cradle an urn in rush hour traffic. Progress is knowing it's not your fault some people can't bear the taste of black licorice.

. . . .

I lay there, said the soldier to the CBC radio reporter, *and my legs were gone, and people were running and screaming, and we could hear gunfire. I looked down. The sand was a sponge where a pool of my blood should have been. I left myself there. Afghanistan absorbed me.*

Six months or so after Liam died, we were at the hospital for another of Ben's preemie checkups: the usual hemoglobin scores, blood pressure, weight, length, head circumference, medication dosages, physiotherapy tests, kidneys, vision, hearing, developmental milestones. We chirped and cooed and he tracked with his head, responding. He was little, but viable.

Next, down the hall, was a meeting to review the details of why his twin was not.

The word *autopsy*—meaning analysis, debriefing, explanation —is a misnomer more often than not, unless the subject was (1) hit by a bus or (2) eaten by a tiger. Chances are good you'll walk away unsatisfied. The doctors may be dutiful and deeply studied but when any human being dies "before their time"—before white hair, before a life is fully lived and neatly resolved—there is no why to be discovered. Often not physically, and certainly never cosmically. We like to think we know all there is to know about the human body, but we don't. Our ability to measure and observe has advanced faster than our understanding of what we're measuring and observing.

"There was a deviation." The specialist pointed to a screen, just like when Liam was alive.

"What does it mean?" Somehow, I knew how this would go. But I asked anyway.

We don't know.

Why are we here, then?

We don't know.

Was he in pain?

We don't know.

Would he have ever been able to communicate?

We don't know.

Will it be windy tomorrow?

We don't know.

Why do you have to buy all the cable channels when all you want is HBO?

We don't know.

Was there a deviation?

Yes.

"When I cut into the brain . . ." the doctor began.

Yikes. Some preamble would be nice. A "Before I get into details, I want you to know we did the right thing" would be nice. I looked at his hands as his words reverberated through the room.

" . . . it became clear there wasn't much left," he continued. "It was just gone, huge chunks of it. Much of it was just an outer film, a jelly on the inside. We still don't know if it was the bleed or the oxygen deprivation at birth or the hydrocephalus. But what brain was there was highly compromised, and the rest of what should have been there . . . wasn't."

The same doctor, during rounds, had once marveled at the birth of neonatology as a Coney Island sideshow called FETUSES OUTSIDE THE WOMB. In one breath, I nodded. In the next, I scowled. But I understood. First responders are the same way—firefighters, paramedics. Incidents anyone else would see as carnage are interesting for them. Carnage makes the day go fast. A great big disaster is a leap into action. To respond is everything they study and train for. It's why they call medicine a practice. But in the NICU, responding is a particularly uncertain business. Its doctors have no choice but to be evasive because tending to premature babies is speculative at best. Some babies that aren't expected to survive end up surviving. Some babies that shouldn't die drift away. Irrevocable damage is reversed. Routine healing hits trip wires, dashing every hope. Surgeons who work in miniature are sympathetic, bless them, but they're mute in the face of desperate parents who sob *Please tell us everything will be alright.* It might be. It might not.

Even now, ten years later, I have looked at Ben and imagined a boy just like him but with half his brain missing, wheelchair bound and seizing, blind and unable to talk, wearing a lifelong diaper, subjected to lifelong interventions and pain. And I'm all mixed up. I am against his death. I am on the same side as his death. We lost him twice: the boy he might have been and the boy he would have been. No angle on it is fair.

> *I miss you*
> *I'm sorry*
> *I'm sorry my body did that to you*
> *I'm sorry I couldn't keep you safe*

God, the guilt for the mothers with phantom babies. For a long time, it was relentless. I could never explain it to the people in my life. *Why do you torture yourself? You didn't do anything wrong. Don't be ridiculous*, they would say, because it hurt them to see me claiming fault. My head knew it was ridiculous, of course. TTTS was a random sniper. Everything is a random sniper. But sorry and sorrow are nearly identical twins.

In fitful sleep, knowing the autopsy results were coming, I had imagined the worst: *We were wrong. He didn't have hydrocephalus and the bleed was correcting itself and you wouldn't have had to suction out his airway every day and we told you he was dying on life support but as it turns out, his lungs weren't collapsing after all. Oops.*

We left the NICU. As I turned the corner I saw a young clinician at the end of the hallway, walking away from me. I recognized her as the one who had put a stethoscope to my son's heart and declared him gone. She had a cup of coffee in one hand and a bagged lunch in the other and seemed in a hurry. She pushed backward through a set of double doors. Shaken, I pressed my nose to the top of Ben's head.

That place is my Afghanistan.

. . . .

"Mommy, where is the other baby, the baby like Ben?"

"That was Liam, sweets."

"Is he in the hospital? Can I see him?"

"He's your spirit brother and he lives with the stars and in your heart."

"I don't have a heart. I'm a big boy."

"You do, goose. You are a big, beautiful boy with a big, beautiful heart. Liam watches you all the time and when he does, he's with you right there in your heart."

"But I don't see him. Why can't I see him?"

"Because he was a sick baby, and he couldn't stay with us, so he went up to the stars where they made him all better."

"Mommy, sometimes I can't remember Liam."

"Oh sweetie, that's okay. Daddy and I will help you remember him."

"What is Daddy going to dream about tonight?"

"Mountains. Big mountains with snowy peaks and black bears all dripping with blueberry juice."

"What are you going to dream about tonight?"

"Fishopia, a place where fish walk around on the land and people swim around in the water and the fish come out in boats to try to catch us but we're all too quick."

"What am I going to dream about tonight?"

"Monkeys on a Ferris wheel."

"What is Ben going to dream about tonight?"

"Umm . . . let me see. How about . . . friendly tugboats?"

"No, Mommy. Ben is going to dream about dump trucks."

"Oh. Okay."

"What is Liam going to dream about tonight?"

"You, sweets. Liam dreams about you."

CHAPTER FOUR

In the Care of a Buggered Psyche

On starting, slowly, to recover in bits and pieces in the years
that follow as loss obscures in the distance.

I N PSYCHOLOGY, the psyche is the totality of the conscious and
unconscious human mind. From Socrates: "My friend, care
for your psyche. Know thyself, for once we know ourselves, we
may learn how to care for ourselves."

Synonyms for *buggered*:

Broken: fucked, kaput, stuffed
In trouble: fucked, in for it
Tired: done in, exhausted

· · · · · · · ·

Our future selves of forty, fifty, or sixty years old whisper at us
to make us weary of the present so we'll step forward to create
what they know is next. But when you get weary of grief—or
when that daily drowning, choking, depressive grief gets weary
of you—it doesn't look like weariness. It looks like rosy cheeks.

One day you'll remember and you'll say, without collapsing: *I
love you, baby.* And you'll sense a nod back. Maybe not from your
baby but from the sky, the trees, the wind. They approve of the
way you tip your hat. Then you carry on to a nice walk, a hunk
of rising dough, a day of labor or lovemaking or weeds to pull.
Grief loosens its grip. Intermittently at first, a vigor or hunger or

need for something else occurs to you. Your body or mind says FEED ME. You rise and stir up a cloud of dust—ashes—little magnetized flecks that say *There was a fire here.* They cling for a while. Then they catch breezes, one by one, until you almost don't notice your skin is just your skin again.

. . . .

The Latin *convalēscere* means "to regain health." When someone has been severely hurt or very ill, they must go through a period of convalescence during which they rest and recuperate in order to regain their strength and health. Synonyms: recovery, recuperation. See also: *Lysis* (recuperation in which the symptoms of an acute disease gradually subside); *rally* (a marked recovery of strength or spirits during an illness); *healing* (the natural process by which the body repairs itself).

—Wikipedia

I don't think we rally, and I don't think we heal. Feeling better can't be muscled into being. It's lysis. You wait. It subsides. It's got little to do with heavy lifting, unless you count patience with oneself as heavy lifting. I remember wishing I could disappear for a while or make everyone else disappear for a while. I wanted to convalesce, perhaps for longer than I'd care to admit, but for good reason. My world was stacked to the horizon with the most oppressive mass of oblivious bullet dodgers.

My own house was safe territory. Ben grew, the doctors weighing his progress to the gram every week. And Evan did a lot of lovely shouting about little trains. They were both in need of simple but constant attention, and the giving of it was a medicine for me. But every other kid in the world—all of them comically enlarged like linebackers, with rolls upon rolls of full-term pudge—would send me ducking for cover. For a long time after, I couldn't be close to any others. I was afraid of them. They were the uncompromised fruit of neighboring wombs, all uneventfully fat cheeks and snotty noses. For a while, their existence felt like proof that parenthood chugs along uneventfully for 99 percent of the rest of the world, landing normal babies upon normal parents in normal ways. Not that you'd want it any different. But I'd see Alison at the market on a Saturday morning: gigantic, glorious, about to pop. I would flinch with dread. The next Saturday I'd see her again, her baby wrapped up in something stylish, everybody oohing and aahing at the soft little head peeking out from inside her jean jacket as she stood with a tomato plant on her hip.

Every ordinary birth in spitting distance made the straw I'd drawn feel that much shorter. Then I'd feel like a jerk, as though I'd been wishing for someone—anyone—to join me at the bottom of this well in the interest of company. Then I'd feel like a jerk for winding up at the bottom of a well. Stupid body. Then I'd feel like a jerk for feeling sorry for myself when I had fresh German bread, two living sons, universal healthcare, my mom's always warm-and-steaming cookie tin, my dad's hammer, and a dining room with a window seat looking out over the creek. Endless jerk potential.

The mother in me—wiser, gentler, more patient—would whisper into the ear of the upset kid in me.

Shush. Feel what you feel but make sure you get some of that nice goat cheese. Then go home and make a pot of strong tea and mow the lawn.

From our bunkers, the bereaved spy on intact people covetously through slivers of blackout cloth, mystified, muttering prayers and profanities. We call on every possible iteration of self to mediate, reconcile, rationalize. Sometimes it works. Sometimes it doesn't.

One of my babies died. One of them lived. I felt isolated among the usual people, humbled among the bereaved. Ben is my subsequent baby and my shadow baby. He filled my arms, calling for me between midnight and dawn for contraband giggles, drinking my milk like a dog with a bone as I sobbed.

. . . .

The free spirit again draws near to life—slowly, to be sure, almost reluctantly, almost mistrustfully. It again grows warmer about her, yellower as it were; warm breezes of all kind blow across her. It seems to her as if his eyes are only now open to what is close at hand. She is astonished and sits silent: where had she been? These close and closest things: how changed they seem! What bloom and magic they have acquired!

. . . They are the most grateful animals in the world, also the most modest, these convalescents and lizards again half-turned towards life. There are some among them who allow no day to pass without hanging a little song of praise on the hem of its departing robe. And to speak seriously: to become sick in the manner of these free spirits, to remain sick for a long time and then, slowly, slowly, to become healthy . . . by which I mean "healthier," is a fundamental cure for all pessimism.

—FRIEDRICH NIETZSCHE, *Human, All Too Human*

Me and Nietzsche sit with a plate of sticky toffee pudding and shoot the shit about free spirit, mistrust, warm breezes, bloom and magic, half-turned lizards, pessimism, and little songs of praise.

"Did you know the word *lysis* also has a biochemical definition?" I say across the table. "It means the destruction or dissolution of cells by the action of a disrupter."

"Neat," says Nietzsche.

At the same time, destruction plus gradual subsiding. An explosion and dissolution of self—we have drawn the shortest straw—the sum effect of which, for a while, is a touch of haughtiness, to put it bluntly. With abuse or loss or sickness or assault or deception or an aversion to loving ourselves or an aversion to others loving us or your spouse goes to work and never comes home or any crap combination of some or all of the above, we grow a taut string of gristle down the spine. With every event it grows stronger. No matter how sensible you are, there's a period during which, against your will, you'll perceive others to be less violated than you, like a rubber mallet on that soft bit of knee. This is the reflex of your destruction. *You are completely, utterly clueless.* The "you" is them, her, him—an "other."

It is true. That apparently less violated person is completely, utterly clueless. She looks at you and might think the exact same thing for a reason you can't discern. You are both correct. Someday, you'll see it, and it will soften you. This is your subsiding.

. . . .

All you need to do is trust your body! Your body knows what to do. You can will the birth you want into being. You just have to want it. Do it and be a better mother, a bigger woman. Do it and be a warrior.

For a while, every gathering of women—cocktails, showers, sex toy parties, message boards—featured a round of birth-story gore. In rooms filled with moms of kids under the age of three, the urge to pass around hospital tales was just as strong as the urge to pass around sleep advice. The well-intentioned "manifest your power" camp plus well-intentioned doulas in training who fetishized birth as the peak of self-actualization amounted to a vice. For me, as the mother of a dead baby, the conversational crush sucked. Forceps, ruinous forceps! Mostly, I found every possible reason to refill my drink. But every now and then, I'd fantasize swinging the story of Liam—of us—like a bat.

Seriously, knock it off. You are fine. Your kid is fine.

Meanwhile, social media was a daily feed of performative pride.

My wife is AMAZING! My wife is STRONG. My wife knows and trusts her body. And so for her—for us—everything went according to plan. #AMAZING #STRONG

Congrats, dude. Crapshoot for the win.

Some people fixate on birth not only as a counter to patriarchy but as a manifestation of female goddessness. That's great, but only if everything goes to plan. Having experienced a traumatic outcome, I felt compelled to reclaim the randomness of messy birth like feminists once reclaimed the word *bitch*. In both cases, we work to shrug at something that would otherwise claim power over us. Shrugging is important. It defuses the violation's ability to make you smaller.

Now and then, because I'd burst if I didn't, I said so. It never went well.

How can you think less of birth—it says so much about who we are, intoned the birth-goddesses.

Only if by "thinking less of birth," you mean that I reject the notion of relying on a crapshoot to confirm or deliver my sense of myself.

You think less of birth just because your baby died.

Yes, "just" because my baby died.

How sad, that you are so shut down from this most important event.

What's most important to you is no longer most important to me. Labor is one day in a life full of thousands of days.

But your birth is the most important event in shaping your life as a mother.

It's not my birth. It's my kid's birth. I am a supporting character, not the protagonist. And the day of their birth doesn't shape my life as a mother. Every day after that day does, whether I am lucky enough to take them home or not.

Your birth is the most important event in shaping your life as a mother, they said. And now, to paraphrase the "or else": *So you'd better make it beautiful and serene and victorious and on your terms. Because if it gets screwed upside down and sideways, you will be forever marked as having been robbed—and your baby, too, who will never forgive you for not being more inspiring and less, you know, unconscious.*

Those inclined to birthwork want to keep the delivery of babies as serene and as natural as possible. And that's great. Yes, there's unnecessary medicalization. Yes, we want to feel like we've got some degree of autonomy on the day we push. The problem arises when birth becomes a pivot point for self-esteem. Birth can't be controlled, promised, unfailingly protected, or made reliably transcendent. It can be nudged along and prepared for, well supported and informed. But sometimes—a lot of the time— even safely delivered, ordinary birth is a gong show. When that happens, we owe it to ourselves to shrug at the mechanics, be thankful it's not 1887, and hope for better luck next time.

I didn't need a rugby pile-on of birth idealists calling me a warrior in the spirit of sorority. Good intentions aside, the wildly overstated significance some heap onto birth is a weight that doesn't make everyone feel empowered and guttural. It makes some people feel anxious, pressured, damaged, and disappointed.

I was not a warrior in the operating room. I was a warrior in the pumping room. I know others who are warriors in living without the experience of motherhood after loss, but who have made beautiful lives and new discoveries nonetheless. And others who were warriors the day they stopped taking birth control, working up the nerve to try again despite the terror. My womanhood is not defined or compromised by one day. Neither is anyone else's.

Scrub in to a neonatal intensive care unit. Tell me and other bereaved parents and parents of children in peril that the mechanics of delivery are the most important thing. Tell them the catastrophic birth of their children—their loss of control— forever marks them and renders their babies (if their babies survive) poorly bonded. Would you?

Does our experience of birth matter that much, given everything else that makes us into lovers, friends, creators, nurturers? Is birth the everything? Or just one thing?

Words shape interpretation. People anoint bodies in hospital beds with words like "fighter" and "miracle" because of our yearning to believe we can affect our fate and the fates of our loved ones, wrapping up the narrative of formative life events with neat bows. But in doing so, they silently demote everyone else who dies, screams for an epidural, or falls apart at the incubator of a one-pound child. We do not exist or fail to exist—or birth "well" or "poorly"— because some manifest it and some do not. This is why SHIT HAPPENS is such a popular T-shirt.

· · · · · · · ·

I would have these episodes—PTSD-riddled conversations around birth were a big one, either participated in or endured in silence—and I'd have to take a moment. The pounding chest, the tears swelling up and threatening to overrun my face, outing me as the mess I feared I was. I'd duck into a hallway, wash my face in a bathroom, disappear to the kitchen until it was over. Either way, I would see nothing but the only certain social prognosis: broken, fucked, kaput, stuffed. My psyche felt buggered to the horizon, endlessly. I was incapable of keeping mixed company.

Until I was not.

· · · · · · · ·

A little about that thing they call "depression."

One morning I sat up in bed and looked around and realized I couldn't see much of the floor. Clean clothes and dirty clothes, mine and theirs, tossed in heaps. My groggy head absorbed this and then imagined what I knew of the other bedroom, the teeny tiny hallway, the kids' room, the stairs, the kitchen, the living room, the woodstove, and the dining room, all littered with discarded remnants of play and streaks of red marker and half-eaten croissants and torn books and crumpled pipe cleaners and runaway peas. Even out to the street, lining the driveway, a tangle of weeds had taken over. They knew someone was living here but she wasn't paying attention, and there's no better place to be if you're a snarly opportunist than the home of a Sad Person.

Four years after Liam died, I left my marriage. I bought an old house by a little creek. I felt like a perpetrator. I had pulled it all apart. We wound up on different planets and didn't find our way back. Now, we work again as coparents, reformed. We're alright. More than alright. Our boys run through the world in leaps and bounds with big smiles and bright eyes. I've got big smiles and bright eyes too, as does he. But the years it took to get here were a storm of wracking, sobbing pain.

That morning, in the thick of it, I sat up in bed and looked around and thought *My house is a mess and I could clean it up.* The mess was no longer a symptom or proof. It was no longer bigger than me. The cloud had lifted, that chemical misfire appearing and dissipating like those in the sky. The cloud that poisons the air, turning all the muscle and slime inside you from a healthy pink into a foul sort of gray, like old ground beef, and it makes you stink just the same. Thoughts, heart, flesh. It casts a film over your eyes so you only ever see, all around you, evidence of how you're unworthy, inept, undeserving of fresh pastries and cut flowers because those are way down the unaddressed list after (1) put those fuzzy leftovers in the compost, if they still qualify as compost; (2) stop walking past that crumpled sandwich wrapper with the smear of mayonnaise on it because it really shouldn't be on the couch; and (3) hey look—ants in the sugar bowl.

For a spell, I was a self-absorbed walking catastrophe. I was angry at everything, angry at myself. *Shut up, trees, with your stupid blossoms and your stupid swishing. Stupid universe. Suck it, universe. You used to be magic and all you are now is stupid, stupid, stupid—dumb just like me.* I spat at everything.

Then, one morning, I swung my legs around, rose from the bed, and began picking stuff up and putting it in drawers. And the stuff I picked up, sniffed, and categorized wasn't evidence of anything. It was just stuff that needed to be put away. The house noticed: *Oh look, she's back.*

. . . .

Getting over it? The words are ambiguous. To say the patient gets over it after appendicitis is one thing; after he's had his leg cut off is quite another. After the operation, his fierce, continuous pain will stop. He'll get back his strength and be able to stump about on his wooden leg. He has "gotten over it." But he will probably have recurrent pains in the stump all his life, perhaps pretty bad ones; and he will always be a one-legged man. There will be hardly any moment when he forgets it. Bathing, dressing, sitting down and getting up again, even lying in bed, all will be different. His whole way of life will be changed. At present I am learning to get about on crutches. Perhaps I shall be given a wooden leg. But I shall never be a biped again.

—C. S. LEWIS, *A Grief Observed*

All of us are learning. Over time we get accustomed to the shock of amputation, of crutches and wooden legs that keep us upright. The most urgent discomfort will ease. You'll walk again. But it's not that simple, is it? It's a strange business to be both grateful and resentful of forward movement. We dread the pain almost as much as we dread the return to ordinary life.

I remember being on the gurney. I remember the way they pushed me and ran, yelling ahead to the OR for the crash cart. I remember thinking: *I might die*, or at least knowing I would never again be who I was, which is a death. My uninjured and whole self would be gone. Lewis continues:

> . . . I once read the sentence "I lay awake all night with a toothache, thinking about the toothache and about lying awake." Part of every misery is, so to speak, the misery's own shadow or reflection: the fact that you don't merely suffer but have to keep on thinking about the fact that you suffer. I not only live each endless day in grief, but live each day thinking about living each day in grief.

Oh, for a nice chowder supper with C. S. Lewis.

It feels like it will never end, this broken state of being. But it does. Or, not exactly. It gets easier. Maybe not easier. Maybe less broken? Maybe the brokenness gets more tolerable. We become acclimatized to sadness and our perception adjusts. Or, sadness is diluted by life continuing on—displaced by other struggles, made softer by welcome distractions and the odd bit of good fortune.

All the clichés are true. Money makes the world go around. Absence makes the heart grow fonder. Glass houses and stones, early birds and worms, laughter as medicine. Want to know if he loves you? It's in his kiss (shoop, shoop). Our little random blip of time on earth is miniscule and precious and rolls downhill with cumulative speed. The older you get, the more you'll shake your head at it. After you are gone—after the yard sale, after new grass has grown over your patch, after the bullfrogs eat— all that will be left are your stories and stories of you, and they fade too. Cue the question that has pinned every philosopher and maudlin drunk in history to the floor: if everything fades, what's the point? Why bear the perfect epitome of hope—a big round belly—to have it go so wrong? Why bother with all the excitement and preparation? Why, for a baby to die? Why, a decade later, am I not tripping over Liam's winter boots?

· · · · · · · ·

Death, however unwanted and unfair, is one of the most effectual teachers. It's right up there with splinters, dull kitchen knives, and woodstove burns. *I happen to everyone. So you better live.*

The second proper funeral I'd ever been to—with pallbearers and a eulogy and people in black—was for my grade twelve prom date, Derek. He would hear a siren in the distance and he'd leap to his feet like a live wire and say *DAMN! How I wanna be in that car. I'm gonna. I'm gonna be in that car, Kate. You heard it here first.* And I'd say *No Derek, I heard it last week too, and the week before that.*

I hadn't seen Derek for more than twenty years. I had moved away. He had become one of the many high school people you never see but still wonder about, like I always did: *Did he make it? Did he get into that car, finally?*

He did. He became an officer of the Royal Canadian Mounted Police. Not long after, responding to a call for help in Saskatchewan, he hit a moose with his squad car. He was killed instantly.

The church was packed. There was no getting inside. I stood in the rain with hundreds of others, with rows of red coats and black boots. I looked down at the grass, at a box with a door and hinges at my feet and a temporary marker and a velvet bag that waited. It was Derek's hole in the ground. The piper led his ashes down the hill, past an unending block of saluting RCMP and paramedics and cops and firefighters. It was silent except for the vibration of hundreds of people remembering him. Then, from where I stood, I heard the purr of Derek's smallest daughter —she might have been two years old—snoring, exhausted, on someone's shoulder from the middle of the family huddle.

(Everything is finite. We should be more kind. Anything else is frivolous.)

At the time, I'd been in the middle of another punishingly self-absorbed phase. I wasn't depressed exactly but in a constant state of agitation at what I figured was my life narrative: *Baby died + marriage died = alone for the rest of my life.* That was the loop—plus financial worries and shallow vanities that never felt shallow or vain, but were.

After Derek's funeral, I went home. I emptied the fridge and scrubbed it out. I pulled weeds. I vacuumed ceilings draped in haunted house cobwebs. I washed the floors and brought wood inside. I straightened the books and hosed down the car and found lost things. Then I took the kids camping. After that, it was wall-to-wall sleeping bags and valley dirt and string-cheese wrappers and festering T-shirts but somehow, when you've recently tidied up, you know you can tidy up again.

CHAPTER FIVE

Hello, Flotilla

How it feels to identify as part of a group with
shared experience and the exhale that comes
thanks to that belonging.

BEET GREENS and portobellos and croissants with dark chocolate on the inside. Seedy rye bread and Munich sausages from the German baker. *Zat veel be seven hundred million dollaz!* He's a joker. I smile, pass him a handful of coins. He adds two orange-almond stollens to my basket, pretending to be sneaky. He won't let me pay.

Evan is running wild, he and his posse with pockets full of change casing vendors for berries and apple turnovers. Ben sits by the sandbox in a patch of sunshine. He is wearing a superhero cape and a newsboy cap and is licking the icing off the top of a chocolate cupcake in slow motion. There are fiddles and hot drinks, and a man yells solicitously from behind a cloud of steam about crepes with smoked ham.

People smile and laugh, friends with arms full of green and goodness, and suddenly I can feel it stirring, that wind that chills you from skin to bone. The memory of what happened and the demotion-by-statistic when you realize nobody else feels a thing.

The only cure is to say out loud *God, this wind. It freaks me out sometimes.* And for someone else to say *Yeah. Me too.*

· · · · · · · ·

The year after Liam died, I went to Edmonton, Alberta, to give a speech at the first Walk to Remember, a memorial event for bereaved parents. *A death parade*, I nervously joked to Bon, my friend and fellow in grief. Not one of those regular-people jokes. Other than a marching band being unlikely, I didn't know what to expect. It was a bright golden day on a green field, with balloons and wishing trees and donations and people embracing. I went every year after that for six years, each time giving a talk from a band shell to a thousand faces with stories just like mine.

The first year, before I knew what this event would mean to me, a young girl stood alone looking dejected, her camera swinging from the wrist strap in her hand. She stared at chalk letters stretching from her feet into the distance along the edge of the sidewalk. All the lost babies were noted along the way, hundreds of them lettered with care by artists. We would find them as we walked. Liam's name was there too, somewhere.

"I liked all the names so I gave them all to her," she said to no one in particular.

"It's pretty," I said.

"Yeah," she replied. The rest came out in a tumble. "Everyone thinks we spelled it wrong but we didn't. It's Irish. That's the right way. She died and then she was born. They said, 'We can't operate, she's less than a pound!' and I said, 'She's bigger than that, do something!' but they said no. She was born three pounds nine ounces, but she was dead, and I said 'told you so.' I just knew. I was only sixteen when I had her."

"How old are you now?" I asked.

"Seventeen," she said simply. "People keep telling me I'm strong, but I just don't like to cry in front of people. I need a picture of her name, though. I can't make it fit."

I took a photo of her baby's name with my wide lens.

"Could I take your photo?" I asked, pressing the shutter as soon as I saw her begin to nod. In that brief moment before she composed herself, I saw her as she was. Thoughtful, peaceful, uncertain. Her name was Shawna. In the second frame she smiled habitually. I like the first one best. Later, after I sent it to her with a compliment, she wrote to me: *I don't feel I'm Beautiful 'cause I feel like Nothing right now, ever since this happened.*

I know you feel like nothing. I did too, I wrote. *Don't feel like you're not okay because you don't understand or because you're not yourself anymore. You don't need to be more or less than what you are right now. You'll probably never understand, but you'll get better at not minding that you don't understand. I promise.*

Is that true, though? Maybe not quite.

Maybe our eyes get accustomed like the never-seen sea monsters who survive at the bottom of the deepest ocean trenches by electrifying the murk. Our eyes dilate, pupils engorged to suck up remnants of light from miles above, and we swim on, uncataloged by social science.

We can all see eventually, I think.

. . . .

I stepped up to the microphone and the field went silent.

I didn't want to cry. A thousand bereaved parents would be the most patient, empathetic audience in the world, but I wasn't there to grieve for myself. I was there to say something—anything— that might lend a little light to someone else in the thick of it. My own snuffling would get in the way. And so to fend it off, standing at the microphone in the heartbeat before beginning to speak, I recalled the sight of Liam's dead body in my lap in as much detail as possible.

As odd as it sounds, that memory has been my silent superpower. When I'm knotted up with fear or anxiety, I take a breath or two and remember the way his face went slack, the pallor and coldness of his skin, the absence of his essence. I remember the hard work of death as my baby endured it and everything slows

way

down.

When I remember him, ego and fear and insecurity—usually a feral pack—heel like greyhounds, perfectly still and subdued. So what if it only lasts fifteen seconds or four minutes? That's plenty long enough to begin.

This—whatever I'm about to do—*is not scary. Not compared to what I've seen. I can do this.*

. . . .

People would arrive early. Some sprawled on quilts or in the grass. Others would move from one place to the next, reading and writing messages on a tree or asking for body art, for a paintbrush and a little bird. There were always so many kids. *A big stage! A thousand balloons! Two thousand, all in great big floaty clumps! Music! Sunshine!* They would eat snacks and run and run. The field would fill up until each balloon had an owner. Each balloon was a baby to be let go. The first year, it felt a bit forced, an affectation I wouldn't fall for. It was too on the nose. But sure enough, holding the ribbon and feeling it slipping through my palm, the wind tugging, the nice lady with the microphone saying, LIAM INGLIS, I felt a strange, tantrummy knot in my belly. *I don't want to let him go again.*

LIAM INGLIS

LIAM INGLIS

All the other balloons waited, the sky pausing like

BUELLER

BUELLER

BUELLER

I let it go and it went up so fast, so high.

The next morning I went for breakfast with Jocelyn and Chris, the organizers.

"Did you feel Liam yesterday?" she asked.

"Not really," I replied. "Did you feel Lincoln?"

"Not really," she said. "But this morning my mother-in-law was driving to the walk and she heard Lincoln's voice in her head, and he was happy. He said 'I'm here, Grammy! Here I am!' and she looked out the window, and there was a baby moose running along beside the car. A baby moose, just out of nowhere, running with her."

"He knew you'd be busy today," I said. "He knew she'd pass it on."

"Yes," she smiled, and we spoke freely and frankly about everything to the clatter of neighboring tables, and the hollandaise was luscious.

· · · · · · · ·

The second year, watching his balloon get smaller and smaller, I cried. In a crowd of people who were all with someone, a long way from home, I had my own little clearing and felt naked in the middle of it. I felt a hand on my shoulder and turned to see Shawna standing there, now eighteen, her face wet too, and she helped me watch his balloon disappear. She'd brought a crew with her this time, with matching T-shirts, CEILI painted on the fronts. The MC called Ceili's name, and a mass of pink balloons went up. I looked for Shawna, but she'd been buried in a loving huddle.

Later, I spoke into the microphone:

Spirits sometimes land in bodies that can only take them so far. How long has it been for you? Speak it aloud, right now, or whisper it, or just remember. How long has it been for you?

I paused, wanting to open up a common pointedness of thought. From the crowd I heard Shawna's voice, clear as a bell. "ONE YEAR."

We're here today to remember our babies, our lost potential. But I'm standing with you to honor you, too: mother, father, brother, sister, grandparent. Every tear, every sleepless night. Every moment of sadness, guilt, or regret at slowly becoming human again. I stand with you in remembrance of who we used to be before loss.

But I don't need to be that woman anymore. I mourn the ease of her, but I'm proud of who I am. I found the emotional muscle to be Liam's mother. He made me bigger, as are you.

Stanislaw Jerzy Lec, the Polish aphorist and poet, said, "No snowflake in an avalanche ever feels responsible." But you will feel responsible. You'll need to inhabit the dark as much as you need food and air. Then one day you'll open your eyes and realize you've crossed from one side to the other, across a boundary you didn't think existed. Recovery is defiance. We have to nod at the blackness and dig to recover our sense of family, parenthood, partnership, hope, and ambition. It's hard work to get to the point where you can indulge again in food and wine and laughter and have it feel okay.

That explosive moment during which everything in the human experience existed simultaneously—love, rage, gratitude, despair—is the same as a bleed on the brain. The heart can't heal from being so stretched, so drowned. It can never go back to what it was. You'll never see anything the same way ever again. You'll pause where you didn't pause before. But it won't always make you cry.

Someday—if it doesn't already—what happened to

you will magnify everything that has you get up in the morning to scramble eggs and get clean and dressed and seek out light and learning and company. That explosive moment is everything nudging you back up.

. . . .

Some years, at the walk, I'd feel weepy at how exposed and resistant I felt. In others, I'd be weepy at how I felt so full of peace. Either way, the tears were never taxing. It was the healthy welling up that happens when the sad story you carry is embraced, his name spoken out loud among so many others who stand up straight despite their own sad story.

As I spoke, I'd find a half dozen faces and cycle through them, one to the other, to see if they were okay and if what I said was resonant. A father would sigh, his eyes wet. A grieving grandfather would nod, holding his daughter's hand. For the sixth and final year, my friend Eve came to the walk with me. On the way to the field I told her how it feels to see people break down (good, necessary), and she mimed me seeing tears and pulling the trigger like a goal-scoring hockey goon. Breaking down is breaking open. If someone else relates, their emotion vents and so does mine. We integrate suffering by sharing it.

. . . .

Thank you for helping me feel like I'm not alone, wrote Selena, who had contacted me out of the blue through shared acquaintances. *I'm pregnant with triplets, but we just learned our girl is slipping away, and we're so sad, just when we'd bought the stroller for three.*

She was a short drive away in Halifax, having heard sad news from the same doctors who had given us our own sad news. We made a date. I walked into the café and scanned each table. She smiled at me, blooming in a way that attracts public enthusiasm.

"I don't know what to tell people," she said, after we'd settled.

"The doctors tell me to say it's twins but I can feel her in there, kicking beside her brothers. I want to say, 'she is here too, and we want her so much, and we're proud of her.' But we're losing her and there's nothing I can do."

I could think of everything and nothing to say to her. We sat together with Ben in my arms, then in hers. She glowed with anticipation as he gurgled, propped on the shelf of her belly.

Not long after that, her baby girl's heart stopped. She would be stillborn with her two brothers. *I had a dream last night I was having the C-section, and the two boys were delivered,* she wrote. *Then they took a young fawn out of my belly. The fawn slowly found her legs and went away. I woke up feeling peaceful for the first time since we were told our news. I am not sure what it means but it brought me comfort. My husband thinks it means she is free.*

Of every cohort of parents, one or two disappear into an abyss. Forever after that we speak a shared language, the ones who fell. It's safe for me to tell you that when I die, I'll magic myself into being thirty-five again, full with milk, and I'm going to cross the good end of the River Styx with one foot up on the bow, mei tai around my waist, to find Liam. To feed and burp him and pat his rump and coo in his ear. This will be my second motherhood. I am not afraid. I will have a job to do.

You look at me and smile.

It's safe for you to tell me that you feel like you'll never leave the house again.

But you will. One day the hole blown through you will have a layer of cheesecloth stretched over it. Then two layers, then three. Sometimes it will tear. Sometimes you'll not even feel a draft, like it's been blocked up for good with mortar and brick. You might resent that protection for how it buffers you from the moment you held your son or daughter.

The hole in you will always be there. I have one too.

I look at you and smile back.

· · · · · · · ·

Kathleen Turner dangles from a collapsed rope bridge above a high gully in *Romancing the Stone*. In that moment, her character is not aware of being in Colombia, in South America, or on this planet. She is only on the end of a rope, with a great horrible empty space pulling her to certain death if she lets go. Every last fragment of her consciousness is focused on the end of that rope, and her grip on it, and the pull of gravity. There is no world. There is only holding on.

You are Kathleen Turner dangling from a collapsed rope bridge above a high gully in *Romancing the Stone*. Now imagine people with bullhorns on either side of the gully are watching you, with commentary: YOU ARE IN DENIAL or ANGER or ACCEPTANCE or NOT CARTAGENA. You want to shout YOU ARE SHITHEADS, STEAMING SHITHEADS, SOMEBODY HELP ME, I AM ON THE END OF A ROPE but you can't. You just have to hold on and listen while robots who look like people lecture you through bullhorns about how grief is a linear process. You wake up every day either smashed on the rocks at the bottom or still flailing on the end of the damn rope with your fingers gone white. And it doesn't feel linear. Not at all. Those people need to quit treating you like a specimen. What do they know, anyway? There is only pain. There is no before and no after.

But there is, I whisper. You hear me and you look and I'm hanging on to my own rope, next to you. You didn't see me there at first.

The only ones who can say with any credibility that grief is linear are others like us.

People who say *Time heals all* or *You'll get over it* or *As long as you get past the anger you'll be okay* are shushing you. Some are shitheads. Others are at a loss and are currently acting like shitheads but think they are helping. From the safe zone, they

instruct bereaved people on the ends of ropes that EVERY-
THING WILL BE FINE.

People like us know the feeling of that rope in our grip. We
are distinguished by the shocking intimacy of this shared experience. Context is everything. Our words are never corrective or
punitive. We are you and you are us. When we sit with you, we
time travel. We join you. We don't lecture you. We were there
too. We are, perhaps, a ways further from our loss than you are
from yours. That's why we can say, sort of, with a sigh for the
exasperating riddle of it: *Grief isn't linear. Except for when it is.
And it always is. But only from a long way up.*

How "time heals" works:

A bomb goes off.

People are shouting, screaming for medics, digging frantically
to find each other through the debris and the smoke.

Bodies are taken away.

The cloud settles.

A bulldozer arrives to push away mangled cars and remnants
of buildings.

A dump truck arrives to take away boulders and rebar.

A broom sweeps up smashed glass.

A Shop-Vac takes away the dust.

The season changes; grass grows. Something new might be
built.

Someone drifts through one day and thinks *I heard something
bad happened here once.*

Someone drifts through another day, a while later, and thinks
nothing at all.

You can't see it's linear when your ears are still ringing or
when you're buried under rubble. The linear nature of healing
only reveals itself much later, after the years required before anyone can stroll through a place where a bomb went off, carrying

something to eat in a greasy paper bag, thinking only *Yum, look what I've got.*

You survive miserably, barely. The minutes and hours and days pass despite you. To spite you. You continue to open your eyes, to breathe in and out. This will be maddening. For a long time. You will have dreams and nightmares, and you will see and hear and sense things you can't explain. You will be subject to unending mental chatter. You will want everyone to stop everything. They won't. Minutes and hours and days will drag you further from your loss. You'll be grateful for the distance and you'll rage at the distance. Time won't care how you feel about it. It goes on. I'm sorry it will. But it will.

When people sermonize about how well or poorly you are recovering measured against Elisabeth Kübler-Ross's five stages of grief, you are justified to shout (or wish you could shout) SHUT YOUR SHITHEAD TRAP. When other bereaved parents sit with you and softly say *It never goes away, but I promise it won't always feel like it's suffocating you,* believe them.

Grief is circular. Until it's linear. Sort of.

What? Seriously?

Yeah. I know.

Will I always be on the end of this rope?

Yes. Until you're not.

· · · · · · · ·

I was nervous to meet Wafaa. It's not fair I was born in Canada, passively lucky, and she and her family had to work so hard and wait for so long to get here. Meeting her made me hyper-aware of all the good fortune I didn't earn—and of the unfairness that her own ancient country, full of so much history and spirit, is now reduced to rubble, her little sparkle-eyed Noor lumped in by bigotry with black-hooded jihadists. Noor is five years old.

"Pleeease," she whined, with the barest hint of an accent. She had known English for three months on the day I visited. "Please I wanna go to Marianne's house. We wanna see the chickens. Pleeease!"

Marianne, my friend's daughter, joined in. "Pleeease!" they singsonged in unison, eyelashes fluttering, both of them jiggling on tiptoes.

They had arrived in an English province speaking only Arabic. *Ce-re-al*, my friend Susy had instructed Wafaa in the grocery store, holding a box of Shreddies and giving it a shake. *See-ree-all*, Wafaa would repeat, smiling. *O-range*, said Susy, holding one up. *Or-inge*, said Wafaa. That was eight months ago.

"I will make you coffee!" she said to me, after proudly taking me around their new house. She chattered on about how she got a rug from a neighbor, and it's lovely, and how nice. And they have a pile of wood to stack. And her husband Ziad has dug out a huge garden! And they have more tomatoes than they can eat. Would I like some tomatoes? Sunshine streamed in through the front windows. A soccer game was on TV. It was her younger son's favorite team.

"Oh thanks very much, but I don't drink coffee," I said. I've only ever drank tea.

"Aah, but you have not had my coffee! I make the best coffee." She swished industriously to the kettle. I imagined there aren't many Arabs who don't drink coffee.

"Cream? Milk? What do you think of my English?" She was beaming, settled.

"It's amazing!" I said. "You have done so much. Are you feeling okay about the winter? You're all set?"

"Oh, yes! We are!" Every sentence felt punctuated with an exclamation mark. "No problem! We get so much sun, you see?"

She gestured to the windows overlooking the beach.

The rest of Wafaa's family are either waiting endlessly in Jordan or trapped behind closed borders without food, water, electricity, or medicine. They have WhatsApp, she told me, her eyes a little glassy. Her brothers, their wives, their children. And then there's her oldest son. He was killed a few months ago. He had stayed behind to fight.

Someday, I'd like to ask Wafaa about him. About all the ways he was strong and healthy and full of ideas. And about how he was killed, taken in an unjust and ridiculous fashion, as war always does. He was her baby. Like I say to Evan, still, at almost twelve:

You are still my baby.

No I'm not, mom. I'm too old to be your baby.

No. Never. Always my baby.

She was making coffee, talking about how they've got the hang of the woodstove. And I was doing that thing, I realized. I was imagining the last time Wafaa said goodbye to her son—leaving him in a war zone—and I was repeatedly shuddering, daydreaming the horribleness of it in shamed contrast to how easy my life has been. Wait . . . was I that jackass?

I forgot how much I have to be grateful for

Then I met you

What with your dead kid and all

Gotta go hug all my everyone TTYL

We all must suffer jackasses of a kind. We all must be jackasses of a kind. Remember that. You might not be so good at holding eye contact with someone who is dealing with drug addiction, mental illness, or c-c-cancer. Divorced people might make you want to throw salt over one shoulder. From them you might walk away feeling a contagion, a frightening relatability, or a judgment, even against your will.

My friend Emily, a Canadian diplomat who was evacuated from Syria when the war broke out, is head of the local refugee resettlement group. She let me know it was time to go. We got up and hugged, chattering about this and that. They talked about upcoming social plans in a mishmash of English and Arabic, Wafaa adding more to her vocabulary with every *How do you say . . .* ‏وليمة‏ ?

My mind was churning. The urge was to say *Emily told me about your son. I'm upset for you and I can't believe how much you've all achieved and I am so sorry the war took him.*

And maybe, very quietly: *My baby died too. Differently, totally differently, and so quickly, instantly really, and I couldn't know him. Maybe that's less painful? You saw yours become taller than you. Your baby was a man. You saw what made him laugh. You might have seen him fall in love. He might have barreled into the house with a sweaty brow, asking what smells so delicious. He had jokes and favorite things, and you knew them all. You had time. Is the way you feel a hundred times worse? A thousand? Does he itch like a phantom limb, too? Can you hear his voice still? I don't know your pain, but I know a tiny piece of it. A flash of it. We have both outlived our babies. It's not right. No matter how old we are, how old they were. I'm glad you're here and safe, but I am sorry your son is not.*

I don't dare equate anything in my life with daily bunker bombs, and I'd never want to put her in the position of having to console me. And so I hesitated. But I related, magnetically, if from a different entry point. The pull to self-identify is strong. Our children suffered and left us in life, and here we remain.

I doubt I'd ever say any of it. I could never make it come out right. But she might be wishing she could wear a lapel button: I HAVE AN INVISIBLE SON. Just like me.

I rail about the chickenshits, and yet I am one, too.

We pulled out of the driveway and waved. She waved back, bending to pull something from the garden. Noor singsonged to Marianne and Marianne singsonged back.

. . . .

The stillbirths, the preemies in the NICU, the bad news at the twenty-second week. The heart-wrenching medical terminations. The loss of a first pregnancy or a fifth. The multiples, the singletons, the accidents, the nonviable complications. The SIDS. Those dealing with infertility or infertility plus any of the above. Within this unlucky bunch there are smaller circles, each with its own unique gauntlet. But that's not all, is it?

At the Walk to Remember in Edmonton one year, a couple came up to me after the speech and said, "We wanted to say thank you, but—" the woman paused, shaking, and lowered her voice, "we're not sure if we belong here."

Their son had lived to eleven years old. From the day he was born, doctors told them he wouldn't survive beyond two years at most. He lingered, but not without great pain for all of them.

"He died a few weeks ago," she said. "We loved him so much."

Her husband pushed up his shirtsleeve to show me a dragonfly tattooed onto his arm. His eyes were glassy. They looked tired, so tired.

"We spent eleven years pushing his wheelchair and changing his diaper," his wife continued, almost in a whisper. "We have this giant modified van and ramps all over the house and now he is gone, and we don't know what to do with ourselves. We don't know who we are anymore, without taking care of him. We didn't do anything but take care of him. We hardly even know each other anymore. But we saw about this memorial, and I just . . . we wanted . . . but we don't know if we belong here."

They were humbled by the thousand people on that field; by the grandmothers, aunts, cousins, and mothers and fathers to lost babies. *Mine died too*, she had said, more or less. *Differently, totally differently. We had more time with our son, though. Maybe that made it less painful?* They related, magnetically, from a different entry point. They were afraid anything they would say couldn't possibly come out right. But it did.

When I was little, I used to daydream in that fantastical, apocalyptic way about the dilemma of which recruitment line I would have joined, had I been my twenty-year-old grandfather in 1939: army, navy, or air force? Would I have chosen tanks and grenades and foxholes? U-boats and torpedoes slipping silently through the deep? Or an aerial minefield, as my grandfather did, flak shooting through his Lancaster bomber until it looked like a salt shaker, as he described it? My grandfather survived four tours of duty. For the rest of his life he suffered nightmares and survivor's guilt, hated brussels sprouts, and forbade the color black. But the choice put in front of him was an abstraction for me, a horror fantasy not much different from imagining which might be a more brutal fate: shark, alligator, or giant squid?

The stillbirth parents envy the NICU parents, perhaps. At least they had a little time, just a little, to say goodbye. Baby might have made small sounds to remember. They saw pink flesh rather than gray. But the NICU parents look at stillbirth and think—hope—at least those babies didn't suffer. It was over before it began. The multiples, like me, sometimes have one that made it. I would consider those who had lost singletons and think about Ben, who drank my milk. I never needed cabbage leaves. But then there's the SIDS parents . . . they might have had a funeral for a baby who was held and known by their community. They have months of memories, making for an attachment and a shock I can't know.

None of it is better or worse. It's all shattering reverence for you. I meet you and I wonder about what you have seen. I wonder how our parenthoods have intersected. I turn your story over and over in my hands—feeling the shape of it, how its volume is unique to mine. I wonder about what was most cruel for you and what was the blessing, if there was one, as painful as that blessing might be to acknowledge. Will I see something of Liam in something of what you knew of yours? Will I see me in you? We seek out this company, looking at each other and for each other, thinking: *What if we had more time? Less suffering? Who else is out here?*

PHANTASMAGORIA: a sequence of real or imaginary images like those seen in a dream.

When we turn a kaleidoscope, we rearrange the same essential elements of color and light. That satisfying little *click-click-clack* of shapes moving into place forms something familiar but totally different. You and I look at each other through kaleidoscope windows, seeing faint glimmers of the recognizable with each twist and turn.

This is our phantasmagoria. Sound it out. Fantasy plus gore. From this angle, we see yours. From another, mine. As we congregate, look how different we are. Look how much the same.

. . . .

I had been walking through the aisles of a grocery store just before Christmas thinking *nutmeg, pastry flour, pecans.* My phone vibrated. An e-mail had landed in the inbox of Glow in the Woods, the online community I'd founded for others like us:

Please help us
Our baby died
(Please bring him back)
(Please wake me up)
(Please rewind time)
(Please make this not true)

Thirty-six hours after, all any of us can muster is an instinctual scream. He couldn't yet formulate the questions that might begin to patch together his reckoning of what had happened, let alone his life after. He was a long way from that. But somehow he found a community of bereaved parents through a search engine, desperate. My heart broke in the baking aisle. What is "help" the day after a baby dies?

Please help us

The e-mail stared at me.

What is this hell

I know. I know. I'm so sorry.

* * * * * * * *

To fall into a black hole is a one-way trip. The escape velocity is so high that light can't even get out. But you don't just disappear. The gravity at your feet becomes rapidly greater than the gravity at your head. Your feet start falling faster than your head does. This is a bad situation to be in. We all stretch when we wake up—initially, it's cosmic yoga. But that stretch continues, and the force becomes so great it exceeds the molecular forces binding your flesh. So you snap into two pieces at the base of your spine. Now, you are two pieces. Since there are no vital organs below your waist, your torso will stay alive for a little while. These two pieces then stretch and snap into two pieces and then eight and sixteen and you bifurcate your way down until you are a stream of atoms descending towards the abyss. The fabric of space and time is a funnel. As you are stretched and split, you are squeezed, extruded like toothpaste through a tube. We have a word for that: "spaghettification," invented for just this purpose.

—NEIL DEGRASSE TYSON, *Death by Black Hole*
(CITY ARTS & LECTURES, HERBST THEATER,
SAN FRANCISCO, FEBRUARY 19, 2008)

The astrophysicist sermonizes about the wondrousness of the physical world, and we call back. His speculations are theoretically sound, but they're implausible enough for us to giggle from the safety of solid ground.

When your child dies, there is no solid ground. You split and split again.

Inside the black hole, you are not able to contemplate the nature of black holes, where you might go next, or what will happen to your consciousness. You can only stretch and split and continue stretching and splitting as this pain happens to you. You might wish for a passing spaceship or infinite improbability drive from *The Hitchhiker's Guide to the Galaxy*—you push the button and turn into a teacup that is then rescued by a sperm whale. Normality returns at a safer point in hyperspace. But contemplation? No. This loss eats all the light, pulling at your body, and gravity is everything.

You say *Please help us.*

I don't say *There is no such thing as an infinite improbability drive*

Or a DeLorean with a flux capacitor

Or a kindly alien with eight legs who can swallow you up, all of you, sheltering you in her gullet as she swims backward through space-time to the moment where everything was still okay.

I wish there were.

I see you, but you are a million light-years away. I see the clothes that still carry his warmth, the pile of laundry still dirty with spit-up. I see your frantic family on a plane, and the two of you clinging to each other.

You say *Please help us.*

You arrived to me through a website in a series of zeroes and ones. I can only watch from a million light-years away.

We are strangers connected forever by shared astrophysics. Years ago, like you, I was pulled apart into atoms and molecules. Like oil in a dish, my specks magnetically drew to one another, almost imperceptibly, until there were enough atoms and molecules for an arm, a kidney, an ear. Until I was myself again, sort of.

If there is a god, she is Time. She is the only interventionist, but she works on an exquisitely, mercilessly fine scale. You will feel abandoned by her until a while later, when you realize she has been doing her work all along. Atoms and molecules, the cosmos. Your son made a little flutter, and they all noticed.

．．．．．．．．

Is she lactating? I asked.

Yes, he replied. *It is hell.*

I sent him to the online library at Glow in the Woods for the article on how to stop milk when there is no baby, but there's not much else to do, is there? Other than *So you have found yourself in this black hole.* I make sure he knows I have been there too. I am writing to him from the other side, reconstituted, though that's not relevant right now. The day after his baby died, he cannot consider life. He is still in the death. He is still in shock, stretching and splitting exponentially.

That is the black hole. I am so sorry you are in it.

．．．．．．．．

The deadliest storm ever in the United States was a massive hurricane that hit Galveston, Texas, in September of 1900. The books that fictionalize the storm and its aftermath are pornographically catastrophic—like books about the Titanic or the Halifax Explosion—making readers wish they could shriek *Run far away! Install extra lifeboats! Step back from the windows!* On that fateful day, the Ursuline Sisters at St. Mary's orphanage tied children to lengths of clothesline to try to keep them together. In the ensuing flood, ten nuns and ninety children drowned in a hopeless tangle.

Is a circle of bereaved people a length of clothesline? Do we

drag each other down? Or are we rafts and buoys? Do we con-
demn or save each other by way of holding this space? I think
the very act of posing those questions means we're fine. More
than fine.

Is anyone out there?

Yup.

I feel so alone.

I know.

I can't believe this happened to me.

I'm so sorry. It's horrible. Just awful.

*People in my life tell me to buck up and move on and I want to
glue their lips to a wall. I know I'm not supposed to feel this way,
but I do. Is that okay?*

*I know it has to be hard for people to talk to me. Especially if they
just want me to hurry up and be myself again.*

I don't know if I can ever be myself again.

I don't know how to process the way I feel.

Am I forgivable?

I can't possibly stuff anymore guilt into this head.

I can't sleep.

Is this normal?

I want to be myself again.

I know. You are normal and sane and the way you're feeling
is just the way I felt, and still feel sometimes.

By seeking and offering company, we form a cohort. We talk
about cremation and share tears over scent-fading onesies, damn
it all. We talk about rebuilding relationships and restarting
careers and heart-opening rituals and being brave and redefin-
ing life and how a film has been peeled off our eyeballs to reveal
the mystery of the world, the constantly imminent peril, the love.
And sometimes we don't talk at all. We're just here.

Together, we are a flotilla.

CHAPTER SIX

At the Mercy of the
Bootstraps Barbershop Chorus

Dealing with family, friends, and bystanders after loss. Many
bereaved people report lost relationships, abandonments,
and toxicity. Sharing is the antidote.

I RENE MESSAGED ME a few months after her son Oliver had
died of SIDS, another episode in our ongoing conversation
from one continent to the other. *Looking for you today. I hope
you don't mind.*

Oh! Are you okay love?

*No, but I'm getting used to it now and don't expect it to be any
different for the next while. The biggest thing for me is the anger at
people who are being jerks. Even those close to me. I can't shake it
off. It's exhausting. How are you?*

I still feel that way sometimes. It's softer now than it used to
be, but when I talk about it (rare these days) it triggers everything
all over again. When I remember how someone called Liam a
"gynecological mishap," it's like an electrical current of anger
through my body just as vivid as a decade ago. Back then I was
in shock, and I didn't have the energy to stand up for myself. But
I saw it for what it was, somehow. I knew the problem wasn't me,
but them. It was a wellspring of self-protection, but it comes with
some pretty painful revelations and complicated feelings. Keep
talking to me. When we connect with each other, we take the
power away from the jerks. That's how you realize everything

is universal. The loneliness, the dismissals. You can talk back or walk away, but either way, quietly rearrange your circle to keep allies close to you.

I feel like a bullshit magnet.

Yeah. Your reaction—naming and pointing at the jerks, even if it's just in your head—that's your dragons stepping up for you. That's your wellspring.

THANK YOU.

Doesn't matter if you give your dragons an explicit voice or not. They will stand in between the soft parts of you and the bullshit. They'll fade when you don't need them anymore, but they'll never go away. They'll always be watching. They'll be proud when you don't need them and instantly onside when you do.

· · · · · · · ·

What is it about the death of a baby that either brings all the bullshit out of the woodwork or inspires otherwise decent people to say bullshitty things? It's a phenomenon.

I have a vested interest and will therefore snap her out of this, they think. Then out it comes. Paraphrased: *Look at the Millers, the family with the daughter who lives in the bubble for her immune system. Or the Robinsons with the alcoholic and the foreclosure. You're not the only one in the world who hurts, you know. Stop dwelling. Think of all the people around you who need you to be uplifting. Be like so-and-so with the Down syndrome boy. She's always so positive.*

My only regret, in hindsight, is that I'd sit there with my mouth hanging open, flies buzzing in and out like Homer Simpson at the control panel of a nuclear power plant. It was too much to unpack. I went outside myself, observing from some other place, as detached as I could be. It was bizarre, but thank god, I knew it at the time. With my mouth hanging open, I'd think *What that person just said is sociopathically awful.*

The corrective/punitive stuff would come from people beset with forcibly submerged pain on the inside, a tidy spit-polish on the outside, and an aggressive commitment to keeping it that way. I was a threat to be neutralized. Turning me proper—sweeping the unmentionable under rugs, like Kleenex draped over a garbage heap (*Nothing to see here, folks*)—would have been proof of everything being in its place, with no place for me as I was.

If you're going to be a Coper—not one of those Non-Copers—you should just forget it. So-and-so did. She doesn't even remember. She never complains, because she's great. She's optimistic! You should be like her. You should be strong enough to pretend it never happened.

Homer Simpson . . . buzzing flies.

I knew what health was. And I knew I had it. I *was* doing well, given what we'd been through. I wasn't curled up in a ball, crying all day (had I been, that would have been fine). I wasn't talking nonstop about what happened (had I been, that would have been fine). I rolled around on the floor with my two-year-old. I grilled cheese and chained daisies. I cried sometimes. Then to bed and up again in the morning for the NICU commute. I'd push those swinging double doors open and step across the threshold to scrub in like Jesse James.

Sometimes, when someone would ask me how I was doing, I'd answer vulnerably. Truthfully. I'd say *I'm upset. I'm scared.* Slowly clotting blood is leaps and bounds better than infection, and I was willing to bleed. Made to live through it again I would choose to be, do, say, and feel the same way with no hesitation. For two months I pumped and cuddled, loving both of those boys regardless of what their outcomes might be. I forced myself to stare unblinking at the horror until I could see the beauty underneath all the wires and tubes because dammit, if one or both of them were to die, I wanted to know as much as I could of their hearts, their eyes, their soft skin, their grunts. Not only their machines and their misfortune.

My pain has always been a clean pain. People with garbage heaps swept under rugs can't say the same. That has nothing to do with me, nothing to do with you.

On the flip side of the forcible bootstraps barbershop chorus is the silent majority:

"What a crummy spring we're having . . . too much rain, eh?" he mumbled as he stared at his shoes. I hadn't seen him since Liam died. I knew he knew. He knew I knew he knew. He stood in front of a wrinkled, gray, twenty-foot trunk spitting peanuts against his forehead with a *shwuck! schwuck! schwuck!* as he shrugged: *Elephant? What elephant?*

I'm being considerate, the silent majority congratulates itself.

I'd always walk away thinking less of you, silent majority. You were smaller than I had thought you were. You were afraid of death cooties. It's years later and I still think you're a chickenshit. You, just as much as the grief-shaming barbershop chorus.

. . . .

Years later, I'm in a café writing this chapter with my shoulders all jammed up against my ears. The outrage—the self-protective mechanism—kicks in, and I wonder if I'll ever be able to let it go.

In my head:

Good for you for seeing toxic people for what they are.

That's harsh. Tolerance for compassionless people is the master class of compassion.

Screw tolerance.

You gonna be this prickly forever?

At least I'm not prickly on the outside. Most of them don't know what I really think.

Doesn't matter if they know or not. You're still carrying it around.

We're nuts, huh? We're all nuts.

Here's a new outlook on ineptitude of all kinds. I'll share it with you because someone shared it with me.

You're at the dinner table, on the street, bumping into people who either know exactly what to say (the wrong thing), or who say nothing. You're standing there with your mouth hanging open. You feel abandoned, shamed, isolated. You might feel like nobody cares. You might feel damn near abused by thoughtlessness.

Here's your mantra: *Jane is doing the best she can.*

This abhorrent scene represents the very best she can do. That's what all of us are doing at any given moment, given our demons and distractions. Our contextual best. And this particular criticism, dismissal, or peanut-gallery correction has nothing to do with you. Absolutely nothing. You need not respond to it, and you need not take it on as something to consider.

So close your mouth. Flies are gross. Flies land on poop. Nod, mutter something, get away. Find some fresh air. Spend your life with people who don't stare at their shoes, and who aren't afraid of the dark.

If you can't get away, embark on a lifelong practice of expecting as little as possible—nothing, if possible—from certain people. You know who they are. What sounds like pessimism is peace. As soon as you detach from the expectation that Jane might someday change her behavior, you're following a sliver of the Buddhist way, the right way, and you don't need to know anything about the Rinpoche to do it.

Einstein said the definition of insanity is doing the same thing over and over again and expecting a different result. It's similarly fruitless to attach meaning to someone else's pattern and to let yourself be repeatedly hurt by it. It's not worth the energy to even inwardly grumble about it. So don't. Jane's pattern will repeat itself again and again and instead of feeling like your face is going to explode, again and again, stand there and say to yourself: *What we have here is Jane being Jane. This is her way of . . .*

Who knows? Who cares? She is unlikely to ever change. Neither will Dick.

· · · · · · · ·

I wrote. I wrote so much. I hadn't yet found anyone else who was bereaved in this way and needed the exercise of trying to find words for what was inexpressible. It was satisfying in the same way it's satisfying to pressure wash something filthy. You animate the inanimate with attention. You hear it say *Aaah*. A surface feels pleasure at its dirt being noticed and addressed, running in rivulets down the road. Even though it knows the dirt—the pain—will collect again. The practice of exposure to light and air is worth it, even for an afternoon.

A farmer friend of mine watched my doves taking a bath in a tourtiere plate. They shook and dipped and shook gloriously, thrilled. "Giving an animal what it needs to clean itself is the most wonderful and basic kind of caring," she said, smiling. "Even for the little ones."

To write—to make any art and be generative, either in solitude or with company—is animal husbandry for dragons. It calms them.

The day after the twins were born, a distant relative came to the hospital with a gift. The drugs were still wearing off. I was unable to move, but I was conscious.

"Here," she said. "This is for you."

I reached out to take it with shaky hands. It was an empty, lined book.

"You can write in here," she continued, explaining. "Since you can't write about this anywhere else. I mean, nobody would want to read it. I mean, you wouldn't want anyone to think. . . anyway. This is so you can keep all this to yourself. Obviously."

Remembering that moment years later, I transport myself back to that hospital room. But not as the Kate with the freshly stapled incision. I am today's Kate, the ghost of her future. *People will say "there's no right way to grieve," but there is,* I whisper to her. *Or at least there's a wrong way to show up, and that's what you see in front of you. Carry on.*

The Kate of 2007 hears the Kate of 2017.

"Right, I'll do that," she lies to the roomful of people, who watch approvingly. She is carrying on. *Good girl.*

I filled the notebook and what felt like a hundred more. I look at them sometimes. I flip to a page and see myself hanging on to cliffs with my fingertips, near hysterical in how alone I felt. But I didn't keep it to myself. I shared everything as it unfolded because that's what was right for me. I founded a community for us, a place safe from mixed company where talking about feeling suffocated helped us all to breathe. I spoke at memorial walks. I made my own light and air. In all kinds of ways I allowed my pain to clean itself. I cared for it. And I wasn't alone at all.

FIELD NOTES
80-Page Steno Book
Ruled Paper / Durable Materials
Double-O Wiring / 6 x 9

February 2, 2016

In a performance hall watching this brilliant, accomplished woman talk about innovation. Feeling quite a bit like a caveman, from the woods by a Nova Scotian creek to shining glass in downtown Vancouver.

What is the takeaway? In business they call it "disruption," and they—the smart ones, anyway—say disruption is integral to positive change. Nothing happens without a shock. She is talking about market strategy and team dynamics and I am listening, mostly, but in my mind, everything she says points to Liam. Not to reduce him to a prop for personal growth. But I am left here without him. There is no bigger disruption. The shock still unfolds, though more gently than it once did. For the rest of my life I will grapple with his absence. Grappling is growth.

I can't love him by wiping his nose. I can't open his bedroom door, see he's all gummed up in his blankets, and creep into the dark to untwist him, clammy limb by limb, for a fresh tuck. I can't shampoo his hair or turn his socks right side out. I can't stand it that he's not here. But would I have rather not known him at all? The mass of this pain is still inside me. I wish I didn't have to carry it. But I'd be his mother a thousand times over. I appreciate his imprint on who I am more than I resent the pain of witnessing his death.

Covering a lecture for a client, I flipped to an empty page to doodle LIAM in block letters, with one star that looked like the hand-cut cookie of a three-year-old. LIAM. It was almost entirely absentminded, his name existing for me somewhere on the spectrum between sacred core and curiosity. One moment I'd been riffing on what I was hearing about experience design and corporate social channels and the next, my thoughts had drifted to him. I was almost a decade beyond him, yet I was adding polka dots to the *M* before I realized what I was doing: noting the disruption that made me.

Disruption. When the twins were born three months early, I didn't have access to a particular faith or philosophical array, but I didn't feel a lack of one either. A hospital chaplain knocked repeatedly on the door, leaving notes about being available. *I'll come back tomorrow at 3:00*, he'd write, and the next day at 3:00 I'd hide in the bathroom until his knocking stopped. But I worried, a little, that all I had was writing. Would it be enough? Was it the right thing, or was it "dwelling"?

Disruption. Suddenly, you're in over your head. You are flailing, panicking. Your faith or philosophy is not the life jacket you'd thought it would be. It is a Victorian ball gown with hoops and layers, forty pounds of ruffles and bustle and a corset designed for admirers, a shallow breath, and a straight back. It identifies you, as long as you're on solid ground. It is your swank and swagger. But as soon as you hit the water, it wraps around your legs and lungs with the buoyancy of cinder blocks.

To be shaken, uncertain, and searching for answers is to be naked. No god has betrayed you, no prayer had gone unheard. No theory was catastrophized into an ultimate test. If you're going to be dropped into water over your head, you may as well be in your skin. Keep the ball gown. It's a part of you too. But know when to let out a seam. Don't buy into everything they tell you that you should be and shouldn't. Make it as easy as possible to find the rhythm of your dog paddle.

. . . .

Don't Complain. You are not so special. Other people have it worse than you. You need to get over it. Don't Complain.

Good Christians don't. I expect the good Muslims and good Jews and good Hindus and all the other good devotees aren't supposed to either, because to complain is to take issue with the grand master's plan. Swishy proper types don't. If you want everyone who meets you to marvel at your perfect manicure and perfect disregard for all emotions in the UNDIGNIFIED category, to complain is to invite the side eye of other swishy propers. The nouveau Bohemian types aren't supposed to either. See also: *The Secret* and viral Facebook memes and airport self-help books about how Positivity! rewires brain synapses to Manifest! Good! Things!

But—

But—

But—

If nobody ever complained, nothing would ever happen. No change, no growth. Like that movie about the town stuck with black-and-white pin curls and pressed slacks, every shirt tucked in and every button buttoned, but with no fistfights and no back seat hand jobs, no midnight ice cream, no musty basements, no French kisses, no gay uncles, no cotton candy cavities, no thrilling risks, no vagina-as-flower art, no smashing glass, no rose cream macarons, no keggers, no stray farts or nipples, no Thanksgiving politics, no caramel wrappers found stuffed between the couch cushions. No complaints. No one to say *Why can't I (scream when I need to / say what I mean / be who I am)?*

We are lusty and outrageous creatures. Our lust and our outrage is the furnace of our aliveness. Complain, dammit. Incorporate this new heat. Your baby died. Complain, darling, and weep and sob or talk about it to everyone or only yourself. Whatever is best for you. But complain. Complain until the heat of it brings you into your color. Gray and untouched is a half-life. The next time your peanut gallery winds up, say it out loud: *Gray is the only true nothingness.* Then walk away. Or imagine walking away.

．．．．．．．．

My mom, cooped up with a toddler and an infant, went to her first quilting bee and found art, meditation, and friendship. I've grown up surrounded by straight pins and fat quarters, bundles of fabric from floor to ceiling, baskets of ribbons and hoops, the hum of her machine, and a house full of women of all ages chatting and laughing and sewing with hot pots of tea and fancy cakes. They were all soft, to me, like my mother. Some were wrinkled and plain and beaming, others wore bright lipstick and hand-knit socks and smelled like flowers and lemon squares.

They all were delighted and occupied, laps heaped full. They knew my name and asked with great interest how school was going, where I'd go to university. They'd pass around stacks of half-finished piecework to marvel at each other's tiny stitches and rare cottons, their voices blending into a chirpy, contented murmur downstairs, their busy hands warming our house.

One day not long after our release from the NICU, with Evan at daycare having a Big Kid Day, I wandered the bins of the Bridgewater Frenchy's—a chain of thrift shops that has punctuated the Maritime experience since before I can remember—with a sleeping, perhaps six-pound Ben wrapped up in the mei tai. I was pulling little long johns from the TODDLERS bin when I sensed someone walking my way. It was Polly, one of my mother's first mentors and closest quilting friends. She has written books and had exhibitions. It was Polly who taught my mother how to sew.

"Oh! Hi," I said, dropping the clothes in my hands and stepping toward her for a hug. She stopped in front of me and took me by the shoulders.

"Oh god, Kate, I am so sorry," she said. "I heard what happened with Liam, and I am so upset for you. It's awful, and I am so sorry. I just can't believe it. How are you doing, Kate? Tell me, how are you?"

Polly, you should understand, isn't one of the particularly flowery ones. She's witty and sharp. She doesn't stand for any fluff, if that makes sense. She's passionately opinionated and direct, so when she said "I'm sorry," she didn't say it the way most people do, drifting-off. She said it how it's supposed to be said. With fervor and agitation.

I can't remember how I responded. I only remember she didn't look away. She was angry for me. She felt it was wrong, backward, and unfair for a baby to die, and she wanted me to know it. We talked a while, had a long hug. She peered into the mei tai to see the top of Ben's head. It's rare to encounter people who say the words *That sucks* with loving attention and outrage. And how lovely it is to exhale like that. I have never forgotten it.

. . . .

Faced with someone who's terribly upset, almost nobody knows how to be. The best people simply say *I don't know how to be.* But they listen, and they try, with no agenda other than to listen and try. The most important part is not the being, but the trying.

When you're wounded from the carelessness of others, remember all the other misfortunes and traumas that would land you, flummoxed and speechless, in some other poor soul's peanut gallery. Because you can't forgive your own peanut gallery until you recognize you can be clumsy too. You might say *But not when a baby dies! My god. I would never say to anyone what people have said to me. I would never call a child a gynecological mishap. I would never tell a grieving parent to "get over it." Never ever.*

I believe you. You wouldn't. But it might not be someone else's dead baby that makes you thoughtless. It might be someone else's car crash and subsequent wheelchair. Once something happens to you, it no longer feels extraordinary. The shock becomes familiar. And so you can't fathom how someone could just clam up and stand there gaping stupidly at you. But you might be the first time they've ever known someone whose baby has died. And they might be reaching. They might say LET ME TELL YOU ALL ABOUT MY BALL GOWN. Or they might have their own pain that they pushed away and tried to ignore, and yours makes them remember it. They don't want to. And so you get chastised.

Even if you are without your child and without any others, other parents—once they aren't so loaded for you (what with all those uneventfully living children and all)—can be a safe haven. The smart ones, anyway. The allies. The ones who put on the tea and say *Now tell me what happened.* The cantankerous quilters. You will find them. They will find you. I promise. They will share with you their own stories of infertility, miscarriage, and loss that might surprise you. Eventually, they will outnumber the jerks.

About jerks. Three things: First, recognize your own gaps in compassion. You've been through a lot, but there's still plenty that is unfamiliar and terrifying. Being aware of your own gaps helps you to understand the failures of others are not about you. *I might do that to someone, someday, in some small way and not even know it.* Every victimhood is best tempered with an inward look for perpetration. This is empathy.

Second, detach from this particular jerk moment—the passive-aggressive remarks on your apparent inability to cope, the pace of your healing, or your mental state—and become an observer. Add every slight, snide remark, or lapse to an imaginary comic strip called ADVENTURES IN JERKLAND. Whatever Jane says, ask yourself: *What would I say if I wanted to have the opposite effect of the shitty thing she's saying?* And take it on as instruction for the next time someone in pain needs you. A good friend calls you, with a shaking voice, to tell you he's just been diagnosed with multiple sclerosis. It is a realm for which you are wholly inexperienced. You know nothing of this suffering. Not to this point. Remember Jane. Reach for the grace she lacked. Add her jerk moment—in which she dismissed you, marginalized you, demanded a Positive! outlook, criticized you for fussing so much—to your instinct of how not to respond. As the future's inevitable sad disclosures, crises, and cries for help unfold, your detached observations of Jane will make you a more gentle, emotionally intelligent, and intuitive human. *Thank you for this gift, Jane. I will consider it. Just not in the way you think.*

Third—I've already said it a few times because it's worth

saying more than once—give every Dick and Jane a wide berth. You need not give them anything else.

. . . .

A caveat: You are alright. You are normal. You are exactly where you need to be. Fiercely protect your grieving ground from jerks and bullshit and other people's exorcisms. Do not let anyone else's opinions or attachments or expectations interfere with how you tend to yourself. That is much of this book, and it is true and important.

But: There is a difference between people who seek to silence or shame you and those who know you well and who may say *I think you might need a different sort of help.* There is such a thing as loving intervention. They may not be wrong, and they may not be insensitive. They may just be heartbroken, watching you suffer. It can be hard to figure out which is which, but try. Take a pause:

Is this silencing, criticism, or someone else's discomfort—or could they be right?

Could this person be trying to get through to me with love?

Might this person see my grief as completely warranted but worries the water I'm in is starting to turn to concrete? Would I be able to tell if I were in concrete?

Perhaps my therapist isn't the right fit for me?

Could it be time for antidepressants / a move / a support group?

In taking this pause, you'll often find you are alright, normal, and exactly where you need to be. The vast majority of the time, your baby's death and your continued existence has simply rung a bell this person didn't want rung. They want to hurry you along. They want this chapter in your life closed not because it will make you feel better but because it will make them feel better.

Your sacred and lifelong dialogue with death is yours distinctly. We are all having the same dialogue in parallel, but it is to each their own. Your relationship with death is yours to forward, grow into, and bargain with. But don't dismiss those closest to you out of hand just because they may be standing in the vicinity of your peanut gallery. It could be Dick being Dick. You know the people in your life best. You will know when to carry on and when to allow their feedback, however clumsy, to prompt some contemplation.

· · · · · · · ·

You've thought it. I've thought it.

> *Oh god I can't do this. I can't get through this.*
> *Everything is falling.*
> *The sky!*
> *We will be crushed*
> *There will not be enough understanding*
> *Money*
> *Stuff*
> *Time*
> *Love*
> *My baby*
> *Oh my god my baby*

Slow down. Pay attention to what is in front of you.

"Black tea, please. And macarons—one crème brûlée and a lemon and a salted caramel. And . . ."

The pastry chef's hand rests in the air over a tray.

". . . one rose cream."

As long as you're paying attention, discord can't exist in the same moment as this. Even if the moment is just a few seconds. Just enough for one good, deep breath.

The sun smiles on everyone, all of us pained and fearful and wanting. We feel so viscerally responsible for failure, lack of control, disappointing others. And yet there are macarons! French confections that are crispy and chewy at the same time, weightless but capable of slowing the spin of the earth. You might be in great need of a sigh like that, the untwisting kind that wraps you in the barest hint of lavender. When your brain or your obligatory social circle is a bloodthirsty mob, find a fresh macaron. It'll go quiet, for a moment.

CHAPTER SEVEN

A Chat with Death

A dialogue worth having: reconciling the irreconcilable.

IT WAS HER last day of ninety-five years. Figures stood against the wall and sat in chairs at her bedside. They were people she knew when they were children, and whose children had children. I imagine it must have been strange for her to leave her house, to be carried out knowing she wouldn't be back. To think *Well, this would be it, then.* It was strange for everyone. She was the dame of the town.

"Yes, there is something I'd like," she replied to the nurse, who had asked. The tale was told long after she was gone. "A rum and a smoke."

. . . .

At her funeral I breathed deep for the scents of an old wooden church: polish, incense, perfume. The ticket booth of god. Pomp and circumstance, a show. Everyone participates, responding when we're supposed to respond, in the same way we smile politely at a magic trick we know is a slight of hand. But I had peeked behind the curtain. As we marked her death we noted her life and when we did, something else was there. I had felt it before. Not a burning bush but a tired, kind accompaniment of energy that doesn't live in a church at all.

It's hard to be around the leaving of a soul, even when that soul has had its due and more—peace, prosperity, affection, decades. But it's still unfair and deeply unsettling to have them go before us.

People who are bereaved—what a petal-soft, round, and whispery word to describe this state!—spend day after day cultivating callouses that might bear the constant pressure of living beyond people we love. With every month Liam felt more distant, fading down the smudgy viewfinder of a pinhole camera, the memory of him breaking up and drifting in all directions. I sat in the pew and the ceremony turned into white noise. In my mind I talked to ghosts: *It's hard to be his mother and not know where he's gone. I'm supposed to be on top of that.*

They heard, but said nothing.

. . . .

Henry Scott Holland, Professor of Divinity at Oxford and a canon of Christ Church, gave a sermon at St. Paul's Cathedral following the death of King Edward VII in 1910: "Death is nothing at all. It does not count. I have only slipped away into the next room . . ."

That there is a next room might be a cowardly hope, but we all share it. Even if we pretend to be too cool, too rational, this wish crosses all cultural boundaries. If we're honest with ourselves, it's one of the most persistent wishes in human consciousness. To imagine retaining links with our most beloved dead—and *as* the beloved dead—eases the burden of being the only animals who know we will die. Cosmology, astronomy, transpersonal psychology, physics, a holy book, Demi Moore and Patrick Swayze. The semantics might differ but the instinct is the same. We cling to the suggestion of heaven, an afterlife, reincarnation, or a five-layer casserole of space, time, matter, energy, and physical laws that converge for the barest hint of quantum insurance. I die, and lo! I penetrate an alternate parallel dimension in which I pass the twenty-seventh week of my pregnancy. Nothing happens. I grow bigger and bigger; they arrive; I push them both out, fat and screaming, as am I; I laugh with my friends about how I pee a little when I sneeze; I walk into the sunset with a double stroller and a toddler.

Some of us wish literally for a god-hosted reunion in the sky, to which more and more adored friends and family come through the door in turn. Others daydream about atoms recycling as stardust and dragonflies. Even the most dust-devoted atheists among us would keep a candle lit just in case, if only there were something—anything—to *Ghostbusters*. If there's a Slimer, there might be something to a contented afterlife. Or unattended hot dog carts, at least. There might be a chance to see what's next. To see again the ones we love.

Everything remains exactly as it was. I am I, and you are you, and the old life that we lived so fondly together is untouched, unchanged. Whatever we were to each other, that we are still. Call me by the old familiar name. Speak of me in the easy way which you always used. Put no difference into your tone. Wear no forced air of solemnity or sorrow. Laugh as we always laughed at the little jokes that we enjoyed together. Play, smile, think of me, pray for me. Let my name be ever the household word that it always was. Let it be spoken without an effort, without the ghost of a shadow upon it. Life means all it ever meant. It is the same as it ever was. There is absolute and unbroken continuity. What is this death but a negligible accident? Why should I be out of mind because I am out of sight? I am but waiting for you, for an interval, somewhere very near, just round the corner. All is well. Nothing is hurt; nothing is lost. One brief moment and

all will be as it was before. How we shall laugh at the trouble of parting when we meet again!
> —Henry Scott Holland, from sermon at St. Paul's Cathedral following the death of King Edward VII

. . . .

At another funeral—the one for Derek, my high school prom date and the RCMP officer who died when his squad car hit a moose in Saskatchewan—I looked down to the grass and saw a little door put there to civilize the hole in the ground made for his remains.

All of us have a place waiting to contain us. A place that's going to be ours when we no longer have or need anything else. Mine is a winding water path of lily pads and beaver dams leading to a gnarly maple that leans out over the water. Eel and bullfrogs and tadpoles and trout live there, and they will gulp me into their ecosystem as they did my son.

Why me? is the king of unanswerable questions. It will exhaust you. It will make you ache. It will make you loathe other people who seem every kind of lucky. I resented them, newly removed to the unlucky side. I peered across the void at them and wondered *Why my son? Why him? Why me?*

Then I woke up one day and realized it's the easiest question of all. Why not me?

All of us are the same no matter how we presume to intellectualize, talk to a god, reconcile, beg, perform, or strive to be worthy. We are all exactly the same. Randomness doesn't discriminate. There's no fault. There's no lack of wanting or deserving. There's no blame. None of us are entitled to an uneventful life. It's long straws and short straws and that's it.

You might say to your baby: *Where are you? Where did you go? Why?*

You are the parent. You're supposed to know these things. Forgive yourself that you don't. You never will.

You might wonder *Why us?*

Why not?

. . . .

I'm not afraid of you, you know.

I know.

I've seen you before.

I know.

I just don't like it when you hang around my family.

Not many people do.

You're just so damned arbitrary.

Am not.

Are too.

Am not.

Oh Christ. Stop that.

Oh Christ. Stop that.

Quit copying me!

Quit copying me!

(Kate glares.)

(Death snickers.)

The whole world wails because of you. Every day. Is that really how you want to spend your life?

(Death pauses, confused.)

. . . .

The Tinguians of the Philippines dress the dead and sit them by the front door with a lit cigarette. For the sky burials of Mongolia and Tibet, the body is chopped into pieces and placed on a mountaintop to be dispersed by vultures and wind. In South Korea, the ashes of the dead are compressed into gem-like beads and put in the keeping of those left behind. There's the New

Orleans jazz funeral parade, the turning of the bones every few years in Madagascar, and Balinese cremation pyres with their wooden dragons. Our culture dictates how to free the soul so it may rest, go to an afterworld, or inhabit a new body. Our culture sets the rules of this sacred work, of asking for and conveying blessings to honor the dead.

How to mourn? That depends. In some cultures, we are all to cry and thrash. In others, the measure of the public torment of women (not of men) is the measure of how much the dead were loved. Unless death is seen as a liberation, as it is in other places, in which case restraint is the norm and crying and thrashing is improper. To be silent is to make the family proud. To fail to do so reflects badly. And so we bear up, as expected. Or we cry and thrash, as expected. Or only some of us. We are instructed how to perform grief by the boundary lines of our birthright, which are just as random as the instructions themselves.

For those left behind, disharmony is the friction between your feelings and how others think you should feel. Especially in the deeply meshed and mingled West, the only answer is cultural secularism because there is no winning. The swank Irish person you sit next to at dinner will think you're disgraceful because you didn't just say *I'm Fine*. The back-to-the-lander who makes her own goat yogurt will think you're suspiciously robotic because all you said was *I'm Fine*. Your pious aunt will tell you you're not trusting in god, which is a vanity and an abomination. *Sway without breaking*, she'll say. *Like a tree.* Which is the same thing your electrician will say, attributing it to Biggie Smalls. Your yoga teacher will not stop with the forlorn, all-knowing gazes. You will snap at her one day to leave your sacral chakra out of it. Your stylist, her hands on your head, will say quietly that your hair is falling out. She will apologize and cry. You will comfort her and part with a hug. Then your sister will tell you, in a flash of frustration that has more to do with her mortgage than you, that you've gotten bitter. You won't speak to her for two months. You will lash out at some people who need protecting and protect others who have earned a lashing out. Your talk will make people uncomfortable. Your lack of talk will make people uncomfortable.

For the bereaved, there is no winning.

How to mourn, if not in Bali? Make a pyre of expectations. Speak what feels right to speak. Be quiet when you need to be quiet. Say you're fine when you're not in the mood to talk about why you're not fine. Do what you're compelled to do. Make someone uncomfortable. You have enough to deal with without worrying what people think of your performance. You have death to deal with, and death has to deal with you, and that is enough.

In the free world, government has to be secular because everyone believes different things. And in the free world, that's cool. Besides, anything other than devoted secularism makes for a legislative and social mess. And so, at least ideologically, government keeps religion separate. It's up to each citizen to worship or not worship in whatever way they like, and we make the rules for everyone based on our inclusive, humanist, compassionate good sense as an ever-maturing and self-aware collective. That's the intention, anyway. The same is true of how to conduct oneself as a bereaved person. You can't please every other citizen. They are as devoted to their judgments as the devout are devoted to their commandments—their opinions about the right way to be.

Your dialogue with death will be one of the most intimate relationships you'll ever have, with ongoing arguments, reconciliations, truces, calls to arms, and late-night heart-to-hearts under the sheet with a flashlight. Some people will think you're doing it wrong, but there's no need to whitewash or legislate your grief so it suits someone else. Suit yourself. Be secular. Be free.

. . . .

A dream.

Skeletons *clickety-clack* their heels down a diner aisle to a booth. "Fish chowder and rhubarb pie, please."

Skeletons prune rose bushes left too long. *Tsk tsk. Gone right wild.*

Skeletons ride bicycles, waving as they pass.

Skeletons climb ladders, wash windows.

Skeletons share seats on school buses, watching you as they rumble by: *You fleshy thing with your juice and bruises and scratches and knocks, twinges and nerves. What I'd give for some fish chowder and rhubarb pie.*

Skeletons were hacked and chopped and pushed and shoved and crushed and just plain withered, fell asleep, here for a long time, veins and kidneys and cheeks left to dry, all the glisten gone. Gone and then the people who remembered them gone and nobody left to remember the remembering, and they look at us, at all of our chewing and swallowing, watching us, curious and hungry.

It's more peaceful than it seems, really and truly. There's no point in minding bones.

. . . .

I feel like I'm always going to be suffocating in my own sorrow. How do you come back from this? Will this loss always define me? Should I feel guilty for not wanting it to define me or guilty because I want it to? How am I supposed to navigate this new life?

I remember wondering the very same things.

How do you find your way back?

You don't. Not like that. But you won't always suffocate.

There's an old-timey cartoon of the good guy magically ingesting a ticking bomb to spare everyone else around him. The hero eats the killer. The bomb detonates, the belly comically expands and contracts, the hero burps smoke. Everyone is saved. After Liam died, I didn't feel like I could speak plainly to anyone. Among some people, anything other than *I'm fine* was unwelcome. Others were loving and open, but I didn't want to make my mother cry, you know? I didn't want her to worry about me. She was grieving a grandson. I didn't want her to fear for her daughter too. And so for all those reasons I ate the bomb. To vent the pressure, I wrote to you. You wrote to me. I found others among us and together, we leaked smoke in safe company.

We took on a feral cat once, or perhaps she was just lost. She climbed up the back steps, starving and covered in burrs. I'd never before heard an animal wail so miserably. I opened a can of tuna and called her Toots. She was a little Maine Coon, if there is such a thing, with thick long fur and a bushy lion's mane, and she was light as a bird.

We took her to the vet who said, "Good lord, this cat . . . this cat is shaped like a bowling pin! Oh, hang on. This cat is pregnant. Congratulations . . . ?"

We paid him money and took our pregnant cat home. We played with her, and she brightened up. We went away one weekend and came home again to a dried splat of blood on the floor. She walked around it shifty-eyed. We took her to the vet again.

"Your cat's not pregnant anymore," he said.

"What?" I looked stupidly at him.

"She miscarried. That would have been the blood."

"What?" I looked stupidly at him, still. "But . . . the . . ."

"She probably ate it."

"She ate it?"

"That's what they do. It's instinct."

" . . . ?"

"If a mammal miscarries in the wild, they need to hide it in order to protect themselves and any other litter. Prey will smell it."

To not clean up a bloody mess is to ring the dinner bell,

heralding your doom as much as we do if we let that bomb keep ticking. The cat knows she is not safe. She has to hide it, absorb it, no longer be vulnerable due to it. This is survival. Like the hero and the cat, we swallow what is dangerous. Sometimes to save everyone else in the blast radius, sometimes to save ourselves. It isn't healthy or unhealthy. It's instinct.

. . . .

I had never seen a dead body before. My baby was my first.

In the same way time becomes its own contradiction as we age—the days going slowly and the years going quickly—death is both the most natural thing and the most difficult. Unless it's in an accidental instant, death is hard work. For Liam, poor love, getting out of his body was a prison escape. Afterward, he looked awful. Battered. I laid his body on my lap for a while.

This will be the last time I will see him, I thought. And so I looked. But I wasn't looking at him. I was looking at an awfully battered shell. Something he used to occupy. His body didn't look peaceful, as some other witnesses might describe a body. It looked empty. There's a difference between peaceful and empty. It was not him. His body was a snakeskin. He had, with great effort, shed it. Maybe that's why people use the word *peaceful*. We see the empty shell, see the animation of the soul is gone, and we are struck with a tiny bit of hope, relief, or confirmation. "Gone" is elsewhere, and there is no more obvious gone than the gone of seeing the dead body of someone you knew and loved. And so the peacefulness we imagine doesn't come from them. It comes from us. We are wracked, but this inanimate thing left behind—the empty body—helps us to understand it's over.

Dr. Duncan MacDougall (c. 1866–October 15, 1920) was an early 20th-century physician in Haverhill, Massachusetts, who sought to measure the mass lost by a human when the soul departed the body at death. . . . In 1901, MacDougall weighed six patients while they were in the process of dying from tuberculosis in an old age home. It was relatively easy to determine when death was only a few hours away, at which point the entire bed was placed on an industrial scale which was reported to be sensitive to two-tenths of an ounce, or five and a half grams. He took his results (a varying amount of unaccounted-for mass loss in four of the six cases) to support his hypothesis that the soul had mass, and when the soul departed the body, so did this mass, leaving the corpse "a soul lighter." The determination of the soul weighing 21 grams was based on the loss of mass in the first subject at the moment of death.

—Wikipedia

Physicists today chuckle. By modern standards, MacDougall's experiments have no scientific merit. The scale he used was comically inaccurate, his sample size was six people (two of whom were not counted due to equipment breakdowns), and his conclusion was not replicable. What's more endearing and notable is that MacDougall tried. If death makes our bodies empty—as so many of us have seen—then where does consciousness go? What once animated what has become inanimate? Beyond our sneezing and coughing and all the bluster of our soft machines, what makes twinkles in eyes? What makes us, Us? What organic material commands our sense of humor, our body language, our attractions? Where do our feelings come from?

There is no such thing as a failure of science. We make a best guess; the answers scurry further away from our assumptions; we iterate; we make another best guess. Every study that disproves a hypothesis lurches us closer to a breakthrough in understanding, as every bad date gets us closer to love. The question of the soul is one of many that makes scientists throw up their hands: *We just don't know. Isn't it wondrous? All we know, and yet there is still so much we don't know.*

You might think scientists love knowing things. And they do. But they love not knowing things even more. Death is a question less penetrable than the Mariana Trench, more infinite than outer space, more closed to our observation than the constant crumbling of mountains. Some people insert themselves to point and say, "Ah-ha! Jesus!" filling the uncertainty gap with a package deal of pearly gates and lightening fingertips. But I love not knowing too much. Not knowing is an opening. Scientists worship the state of not knowing like the sacred gift it is: when we get even a small sense of just how much we don't know, we get something marvelous: humility. A carrot on the end of the stick of human growth. Will we ever catch it? Nope. But the chase is more important than the catch. The chase is what makes us dream. Isn't it wondrous?

They know how the brain works—a circuit board with crisscrossing currents like a map of the London Underground. Shivers and yawns, the fight or flight instinct, whatever it is that keeps our chest rising and falling when we're asleep. But they also have no idea how the brain works. How memory gets into our bones. How we have premonitions. Whether you believe in the paranormal or not, you've had a premonition, or your aunt has. I knew my babies would be born soon, and in peril, and I didn't know I knew until after. *Last night I dreamed my babies were born too soon.* Where did that dream come from? What was its purpose, since no warning could have averted the outcome?

Months after our release from the NICU, we were walking in the city. A man approached, waving, and shook hands with my husband. The two of them chatted while I smiled politely. I didn't know him. I looked up at the trees, at the leaves swaying. I thought about errands, getting home through traffic.

Then I smelled morphine. I startled and looked from one face to the other and back again. They were talking about weather, sports. The scent grew stronger—almost enough to make me interrupt, but I was too stunned. The pungent chemical was dripped through Liam's scalp intravenously as he died, the contraption a third participant as I brushed my lips to the fuzz on the top of his head. I know the cold squirt and metallic tang of its administration. The battleground angel at his death. I know it, and it knows me.

They carried on as I inhaled frantically, confused. He said *Nice to see you* and we said goodbye. As the man went along down the sidewalk, the cloud left with him.

"Did you smell that?"

"Smell what?"

We walked a while more.

"Do you know who that was?" he said.

"No. Should I?"

"That was your anesthesiologist."

The battleground angel at his birth. I remember a blue mask leaning over me upside down, inches from my face, telling me I would feel cold. I never knew who he was. But my body did. He was attached to my disaster, our disaster, a straight line from him to me to Liam. Something in me knew it.

We have always perceived what eventually turned out to be science as sorcery. But I want this particular sorcery to stay. I don't want my understanding to penetrate this magic, to ruin the mystery of gut instinct and muscle memory. It's like people who don't dare ever meet their heroes. If Bon had met David Bowie, she might have heard his stomach growl. Her Ziggy Stardust might have gone POOF. Where does the soul go? Sorcery. What comprises MacDougall's twenty-one grams? Sorcery. How can I still feel the grit of hospital under my skin? Where does the blind memory of trauma live, if not in my conscious brain? What other, more primal thing lives in the gut or at the base of the spine? Are we rooted by more than the cerebral? Could those roots be stronger than what we think we know? Is memory cellular? *Goodnight moon, goodnight plasma. Goodnight membrane, cytoplasm, nucleus.* Are we more an environment than a being, a community of blood witnesses? Was one of them screaming on the sidewalk that day? Are we our own keepers and guard dogs?

Don't tell me. *Shh.*

. . . .

Someday, you'll get as far as suppertime before consciously remembering. You'll be adding butter to rice, worried you've burned the almonds again. Your mind will chatter, as minds do:

Power bill

Snow tire appointment

Pretty sunset

Meeting tomorrow

Skype keeps crashing

Suddenly, putting on an oven mitt, you'll remember you ate a bomb.

The baby died

The timer will ding. You'll open the oven door and take out the frittata. You'll fill plates and sit down to eat and realize you've gone one whole day without actively thinking about what happened to you. Until the almonds begin to over brown:

That was me. That was us.

But then, *Wow. What time is it?*

6:12 p.m.

It's been all day. I haven't thought of it once, and it's been all day.

Loss defines you as much as everything else. Sickness, love, career, marriage. Things coming apart and things coming together. Every relationship, pothole, and happy coincidence. Right now, loss has overwhelmed everything else. Someday you'll remember, and you'll wait for your eyes to get hot and glassy. But they won't. Loss will be a big thing, but still, just one thing. The first time it feels this way, you might feel strange. But at some point, we all have to give permission for our baby to be lost. Disbelief gives way to giving way. Your child is not with you. And you'll say *Alright, baby.* This is the great and fearsome letting go. This is you, as a parent, saying *Be good, wear your mittens, and don't forget to bring a snack.* This is *Bye-bye, sweetheart.*

This is your active care of that lost soul, and of you in the losing. This is you no longer smelling like fresh blood, no longer quite so vulnerable to prey. The bomb is still in you, but your body has grown around it. This is phantom parenthood.

You will eat frittata with Reggiano that cost too much. It will be delicious. You'll sip a glass of wine, balancing a plate on your lap. You might be alone. You might not. But you'll remember, and you will not fall in a heap.

You'll say *Alright baby, alright* and turn the oven off.

Your stress will change: from grief triggers and panic attacks to the fact that your car smells like compost. Compost with fabric softener tucked under the front seats. Perfumed compost. *Do I still qualify as an adult with a car that smells like this?* Income tax season plus the fresh anxiety of coparenting made my hair fall out in clumps. It was the regular, cumulative bumble of daily life that brought on the asthma. Not the baby death. What sense does it make? I held my child as his heart stopped, but dating as a forty-year-old is what had me gulping into paper bags every twenty breaths. How could I outlive Liam and be undone by the prospect of Tinder and a solo mortgage?

"I'm eating a metric shit-ton of butter," I wailed to someone. "I can't see the butter without my glasses. Everything is getting worse. Age! Years! Passing! My hair is falling out. I can't breathe."

"I suggest Reiki," the someone said. I went for Reiki.

Is it working? I don't feel anything. WAIT. I feel heat. She's all hot handed. Heat. Oil bills. TV sucks. Who watches sitcoms anymore? I can't forget to pick up that thing on the way home. Things. Ugh groceries. My car. The engine light is on. Is it just that Volkswagen thing or is it really something? Brakes? The exhaust? Daphne. I have to call Daphne. Whoosh. I feel a whoosh. Wait. What? Her hands. Plane. Ticket to North Carolina. Hurricanes. It's almost . . .

"You need to quiet your mind," said the Reiki lady. "And uncross your arms and legs. You're blocking me."

My mind quieted, but only sort of. It whispered to itself at double speed, just like everyone else's.

CHAPTER EIGHT

Anniversaries

Almost more than a birthday, bereaved parents can't help but mark a death day. An exploration of how grief changes and softens over time, as it has for me on June 15 of every year.

YEAR ONE

A FEW WEEKS before one year to the day the twins were born, I fall apart, but oddly. Not only with the pain of losing him but with tolerating the minutia of life after losing him. I lament everything. How to take time away from paying work to write a novel after losing ten thousand dollars buying and then immediately selling an unnecessary minivan. How to lurch on ahead, getting older. How to sleep without thinking. How to shake this angry pallor.

One year in, I am exhausted by the grief. The pressure to be in a state of constant spiritual vigilance and remembrance is a weight on my chest. There is too much to remember, too much to shrink from. Too many anniversaries: the first day he died (the day he was born), the second day he died (the day he died again), and the six weeks in between. His heart surgery, his steroid-fueled bloom, the day his brain began to flood. And June 14: the day they tried to fix it with a shunt in his head, and it failed, and the flood got worse, and the doctors finally decided (*he* decided, they said) he had had enough.

I feel the same way.

Year Two

My baby died. Where's that gallon of Varathane? Time for another coat.

Two years after it happened, I hide from it. My brain is a loop-ing replay of what might have been, as it always is: The preg-nancy carries on and we are safely delivered. I have three sons. Or the pregnancy does not carry on, and everything explodes as it did, but Liam's hydrocephalus is manageable. Our life is one of power wheelchairs, vans with hydraulic lifts, lifelong diapers, repeated brain surgeries. I have three sons. This is how I hide from what really happened. Two years later, I am glad to be busy and I am ashamed of being glad to be busy. I don't know what to do with myself. To think of him, even fleetingly, triggers the only words I have: *I'm sorry. I'm sorry we've gone on without you.*

Eighty-five percent of lost mountain climbers die on the way down from the peak. Not on the way up. On the climb, every adventurer gone before them cheers in spirit. But on the way down, those voices go silent. Ghosts fall after the peak. On the way down, you are fatigued. Your legs are throbbing and you're oxygen depleted. Your mind starts to play tricks. You're hemmed in by impending weather and night. On the way down, you can't see footholds. Outcroppings are more likely to crumble. We land more heavily, with less grace. We fall.

In the first year, everybody knows. There is an odd sort of glory in making it to the one-year mark, the impossible peak. People say *We remember* and *You're so strong.* In the first year, your continued existence is a spectacle, a wonder. Your loss was the foremost thing. But by the second year, this social contract has faded. People will think all kinds of things when they see you and perhaps not at all about your baby. Now, other things are more prevalent. There is new drama, yours and theirs. They want to move on. You want to move on. The only person who feels awful in this longing is you.

It's lonely on the way back to regular life. Every step is painstaking. Returning to base camp, let alone to a hot bath in the village, is many times slower and more perilous than the climb.

YEAR THREE

Three years after the night they were born, I can't sleep. *Three years ago right now . . . he was alive.*

What happens next is strange. I am not flooded with the nightmarish memory of how he looked that night, or with the conditions of his white-knuckled diagnosis. I am flooded with the way you feel when you're twelve years old, waiting at the top of the stairs on Christmas morning.

He was alive!

Happiness, as if it had all turned out some other way. Unreasonable, irrational happiness. My brain says *But he was in pain and he died.*

And my heart says *Oh, shut up.*

And my brain says *You're not supposed to ever say SHUT UP to anybody. It's the rudest thing you can ever say.*

And my heart says *I'm tired of all your death and purpleness and misery. He was here! He was here. I made him and he was beautiful, and knowing him, even a little, was sublime, and I don't care what you say.*

Three years after, in the middle of the night that marked the moment just before everything went wrong, that he was ever here at all makes me feel like the luckiest unlucky mother ever. My brain walks away, shaking its head. My heart spins around giggling in a field of sun-drenched daisies.

· · · · · · · ·

Everything is new and dewy and fresh. I roll down the window along a green stretch. We live in the country where it's quiet except for small birds and rustling leaves and the churn of the ocean. A dump truck passes with a clinking of chains and an airy *whomp*. I look into the side mirror to see a teenage boy walking on the shoulder of the road, with boots and a pack over one shoulder. He's on his way somewhere. It's Liam. I blink. The boy vanishes. Where he was walking there is now a small wheelchair left out on the side of the road along with unwanted sofas and lobster traps like it's spring cleanup. I blink again.

I try to imagine how he might have survived, how he might have been alright. These are separate worlds. In both, I love him. But neither can be true here, where I am.

Every year, the night of June 14, Liam will die again. For the twelve hours it took, I will cry. Every year, the next morning, I will make a bleary pot of tea. I will light a fire in the woodstove and I'll just sit.

Was it true?

It felt true.

It felt like we weren't alone.

He went somewhere. Something took him. I don't know where.

I felt him lifted from his body.

I don't know what it was, but it was true.

My uterus drowned one baby, drained the other, and exploded. I could get lyrical about it. I could presume to forgive it, except my womb is a mouthy mofo who thinks anthropomorphic reconciliation is for pussies. We can't figure our way out of an experience like this. We can't muscle the grief of loss to "heal" any, more than an alcoholic can outsmart his alcoholism. We either integrate it, humbled, or we don't.

You will encounter new things and good jokes. You will visit unknown places, putting geographic and chronological distance between you and the site of your explosion. You will learn to surround yourself with people who understand that occasional sadness is not about them, and who never begin sentences with *You should* . . . unless they end with . . . *come over 'cause I just made soup.*

Loss, like motherhood, never ends. He will always be mine. He will always be gone. This specter will always be attached to me. I'll never be sure which one of us is holding the leash.

Woof.

Year Four

I lie on my back with one leg bent, foot propped on the other inside knee in horizontal tree pose. I sprawl under the familiar heaviness of my duvet, with the luxury of line-dried sheets I didn't grow to appreciate until I grew to appreciate other grown-up things like capers and gorgonzola. Just before sleep, I curl into a ball. Left hand cupping the right shoulder, right hand cupping the left. I am a knot. I wake up that way feeling stiff, like I'd been only pretending to sleep all night long.

Poor body. Poor faulted thing, host to this ungrateful creature who never noticed you. Not until you slipped, body, and when you did, I cursed you, never mind the almost four decades of perfect uneventfulness you gave me. You are aging. You ache, I think grumpily, for no reason. You decline, reminding me of what's inevitable, and I resent you for it. You lose the subtle elasticity I didn't know I had until it began to be lost. The feet on you, body, grow gnarly in that way I swore they never would, and the heart too, and the mind.

Starting when we're young, we abuse our bodies. We deny them sustenance, care, worship. We think our bodies owe us something. Functionality, at least, if not also attractiveness, svelte lines, the right kind of curves and not the wrong.

But it's charmed. All of it.

Even what you diagnose, in your arrogance, as unpleasing: *Here is where I fail.* You grab it, a fistful of evidence. Sometimes hating it righteously, not only vainly, on behalf of the other soul or souls it failed in addition to your own.

Try, with every step: *Thank you.* Every scent and stretch and squeeze and yank and knock and growl. *Thank you.*

Year Five

On the fourteenth of every June—marking the beginning of his end—I feel like I'm not doing, feeling, writing, or saying the right thing. I get quiet and notice his absence. *Did that really happen? Well, yes. It did.*

I used to feel an odd sort of peace. I had loved him. I held him. I was sad, but it was a functional sort of sad. But in the fifth year, I dismantle his family. His father and I separate. This stirs up so much pain, and in a dark way. Like in dumb horror movies where cheerleaders and quarterbacks evade death only to have death hunt them down by way of fence-post impalement or swarm of bees or falling gargoyle or combine harvester. All that golden sorcery the year after he died was my evasion. Trees spoke to me and Liam spoke to me. I felt watched over. Ben needed milk, Evan needed trains. Things grew. But five years after, the dark thing wants its reckoning. I see my name on divorce papers and it says right there, brutally: PETITIONER. What I have done feels like I set him adrift, and his father and brothers too, no matter how amicable we manage to make it. I become a full-time catastrophizer, and for plenty of reasons. I am fundamentally more to blame for this than I ever was for his death.

This year, I go in the canoe again to see his place. It's pretty in there, always calm. I touch his water to my lips. I run my hand through the pebbles. His urn is under there somewhere, right there, tucked in. I feel clumsy and ashamed. He feels farther away than ever. I stay a while, then paddle away.

Year Six

The kids are shimmering with happiness and the sun smiles through the window and the onion rings are crispy and the root beer is a two-handed frosty mug and we spin on the stools and the ketchup is splurty and I am in love with the moment. Then I eat the whole tray. Now it's full-system shutdown. Ergh. I drive home, the boys chattering in the back seat.

It is the sixth anniversary of the day he died, and I feel gross. Onion-ring gross.

There's a Robert Frost poem about flowers getting pelted by the rain. I could read that and think about it for a while, but it's time to go pump ten pounds of Agent Orange into that anthill and watch them scatter.

It is the day he died. I don't know what to do about that.

Year Seven

I am sitting in the Calgary airport, waiting for the flight home, listening to Simon and Garfunkel's "The Only Living Boy in New York," thinking dreamily about Blackfoot drums on the prairie.

I look down at the plane ticket in my lap for my seat assignment and see the date. June 15. . . JUNE 15. In realizing I had forgotten entirely—missing the night-before anniversary of when they took away his ventilator and our death vigil began, missing the 7 a.m. mark this morning of the moment he had died—my lips swell, my cheeks swell, my eyes grow hot. I can see myself sitting here. I can see I've forgotten. The past six weeks have been a blur. I went to Alberta to launch a new novel. During the tour, Alberta was overwhelmingly big-sky large. I shook with nerves in a motel room on the Blood reserve the night before going to Stand Off, a real-live place in my imaginary story. I gave workshops and read to the kids who live there, encouraging them to write and hoping they wouldn't mind that in my book, Bloods were friends of airborne eco-warrior pirates. I went from school to school, driving past grain elevators and cowboys in silhouette. I got out of the car to rest at a gorgeous view of a ranch spilling off in every direction like an ocean of tall grass, and a thousand-pound bull came close, just the other side of a fence, and pawed the ground at me. The days blew by. I made money and spent it. I ordered food and ate it. I forgot the day of my son's death.

In Stand Off, rez dogs cruise the streets like Danny Zuko's T-Birds in *Grease*. A pack of them ran to me in front of the high school with tongues lolling, covered in mud and burrs, and I stood still as they tumbled toward my body at top speed. The leader, a bushy black bear, took a running leap and landed with his paws on my shoulders as if to knock me down. I braced myself and stood still, his breath on my face and his nose touching mine. Then he used my shoulders to stretch like *aahhh*, and I fell in love with him instantly, with all four of them. I fantasized about bringing them home on the plane. I wished I could buy each of them a seat and a meal in a plastic bento box. I gave them a stale blueberry muffin from the car and imagined living my life under a shaggy pile.

Snarling packs run at you, smelling you from a long way off. Like Rilke's dragons, perhaps the feral dogs in our heads only want a gas station muffin and a scratch from someone who doesn't mind the fleas. Everyone needs love. The ghosts, the posses of wild mutts. They'll take it when you give it, but they don't hold it against you when you've just got to keep walking.

YEAR EIGHT

I appreciate how art rearranges the impossible into a shape we can absorb.

How lovely he was, though he looked terrible, you know? He was lovely.

How the light sweeps across the woods at dusk and the shadows get long and everything is golden and everything shout-whispers: YOU ARE ALRIGHT. SEE! LOOK! PRETTY! I hear her now. My conversation with nature started when he died and it has never stopped. I am glad for it.

How things were always worse than I knew.

How things were never as bad as they felt.

How lucky I was. How strong I was. How unafraid I was. How certain I was that I was none of it.

How Irene called me from France the day after her baby didn't wake up from his nap. How her crying sounded on the phone from across the ocean. How I didn't flinch. How none of us flinch. Not for each other.

How the only thing I feel now, mostly, is just love for him. I remember the day he was born. I remember the day they took away the oxygen and I saw his face for the first time. I remember the day a nurse gave him the only bath he ever had, gently washing away the adhesive and remnants of intervention, leaving him so fresh and so nearly-normal it made me wonder if he might survive after all. I remember his last day when all the color drained from the world. The shame is faint now. It's there but other voices shush it. Strong, healthy voices, all mine.

YEAR NINE

I make pies, cookies, chili. We bring wine, San Pellegrino, French baguettes, brie, Castelvetrano olives, and dark chocolate. We wander the lodge for musty old board games and books. We eat big breakfasts and have lunches on the porch, nibbling and sipping and exploring all afternoon. The boys fish for little rainbow trout, squealing with delight and then throwing them back. We skip rocks and play horseshoes and go on little hikes and bike rides around the point. We walk along quiet dirt roads on quiet lakes in the quietest part of the province, and birds sing. Water gently laps against the shore outside the window of our cabin, which smells not only like wood smoke, but the smoke of generations of fires.

Nick and I—a "we" for the first time in a very long time, as I spent several years single and patching myself back together until I met him—bring the boys to the spot where Liam's ashes are. Evan and Ben have heard about it for years, though I don't say he rests there, exactly, because I don't believe he does. The spirits at this old lake lodge are of me, of his father smashing the top off the urn with a Swiss Army Knife because the stopper got stuck. We set what was inside loose onto the surface of the water, some ashes penetrating the tannin to drift and float through lily roots, others skirting the surface like dancing water striders. When I come here, I see us, imprinted. I see our intention. I time travel to when he was closer to me. I touch the ancient maple tree that drapes green limbs and fingertips over the most peaceful and kindest water in the world, the creature that marks the spot.

There is the usual bluster of getting everyone into the right shoes, swim trunks, sunscreen, life jackets. We set out from the cabin dock and watch for turtles, lilies, and bullfrogs. We haul both boats over a dam, crunching sticks under rubber boots. *Sorry, beavers.* We paddle until we can see the opening, camouflaged by trees: the little waterway that grows smaller and shallower as it winds and curls toward a wooden bridge deep in the forest, tall grasses touching our shoulders on either side as we float silently in the sunshine.

Liam's tree is the crown of this place, the watcher. I bring my sons to her, and the man I will marry, when I marry again.

I reach up to grasp a limb, an anchor above us to keep us in place. Nick holds my boat to his. We tie ropes and get out, stepping into warm, knee-deep water and pebbles formed into waves, hills, and dunes by the current. My bare feet sink a little into them, into the burial ground. His urn is under here somewhere.

I sit in the water, soft and sparkling. It swirls around me. Evan dangles his feet. Ben stays in the canoe to look up into the tree, almost shy of it.

"She is such an old tree, isn't she, Ben," I say. "Just like Mother Nature."

He smiles. "I have something I want to leave for her."

In his hand is a white water lily found drifting off its pad. He reaches up, putting the flower on the maple's limb, and he looks at me.

"That is to say thank-you."

He has his own dialogue with death, too. He remembers. *Liam told you all his secrets*, I have always told him. *They would put you together, you know, in the same crib, and you would suck on each other's fingers.*

We sucked on each other's fingers!?

You did. He giggles, always.

We race back, shouting and howling while we paddle, "Heave! Heave! Heave!" and "Land ho!" We sleep heavily and wake languorously. I get out my favorite journal, big and broad with soft, silky German paper, and I write about the tree, about nature and how she tended—and still tends—to my lost son.

We have the best time, a time soon transcended by other best times. I am not hiding anymore.

YEAR TEN

In June of the tenth year since Liam died, I was editing this book to deadline. Reading aloud, consolidating, time traveling, deleting, crying, responding to editor queries like *What do you mean by "Me being Relic from* The Beachcombers *is low-hanging fruit", can you clarify?* Fretting about getting all the nihilisms right. And I completely forgot the day of Liam's death. Not like a few years back when I looked down at my plane ticket and realized it was the day, that day. I forgot-forgot. I didn't realize it had passed until three weeks after.

So this is ten years, you dick

Contemplation and a reprimand—what a shit mother I am to him!—then a glimmer of relief that I am far out enough to be afforded the privilege of forgetting. Although, of course, there is no "forgetting." I will never and wouldn't want to. I remember all the time, my laborious mosaic, my illumination, and I miss him constantly. But June 15, the day, blew by with nothing but work deadlines and a grocery list. Then the next day and the next week and more blew by, too. I feel all kinds of ways about it.

"I had never considered bereavement as a permanent state," wrote Dave, a friend and bereaved dad when I told him in passing. "Life is so fleeting. We gotta make as much meaning as we can with however much time as we get. One of my takeaways from Tikva's life is I'm now reluctant to put experience in piles of 'desired' and 'undesired.' I can't see allowing myself to twist like that, susceptible to changing winds out of my control."

He added a smiley face. I thought about that, sending out, again, for the thousandth time, gratitude that I know these people. People like us.

. . . .

Other bereaved friends plant trees, write letters, cry. I am never sure what to do. I might wonder if I should write something. Burn something. Make something. Put something into the creek. Bake a tiny cake and throw it as far as I can into the bay after saying something. Sometimes I go to the old maple. Sometimes

I am alone. Sometimes not. The struggle is always that I should do it properly, but there is no properly. In recent years, muscle has been meaningful. When I didn't know what to do, I picked up a crowbar and pulled the old siding off the shed while squirrels darted back and forth across the yard, and I said nothing at all. Just sweat.

What I know now: the anniversary of his death is one day out of three hundred and sixty-five in a cycle full of thoughts of him. A well-timed crowbar is just as valid a meditation as anything else that gongs.

. . . .

How do we mother invisible children after our bodies have stopped smoldering? If I don't paddle to the place where we left his ashes, am I standing him up?

The phantom teenager of what he might have been rolls his eyes. *Ugh, Mom.*

It's what mothers do. We worry.

(Phantom kiss.)

. . . .

It won't be a particular day that will crush you. It'll be next Tuesday or September 18 or New Year's Eve five years later, when you're in a pub with friends. You'll see yourself in the mirror and something deep inside you will shriek DEAD BABY and you'll go from adorably drunk to insufferably maudlin in an instant. And you'll wind up crying on the toilet.

> The most beautiful experience we can have is the mysterious. It is the fundamental emotion that stands at the cradle of true art and true science.
>
> —Albert Einstein, *The World As I See It*

Cry on the toilet, insufferably maudlin! Einstein's apparition fruitlessly tries to wipe mascara from your cheek.

I am fundamental

Say it.

I am at the cradle of true art and true science

I am beautiful

Well. You look terrible. You're crying in a pub toilet. But you're beautiful.

> No anguish I have had to bear on your account has been too heavy a price to pay for the new life into which I have entered in loving you.
>
> —George Eliot, *The Mill on the Floss*

Blow your nose.

> The arts are not a way to make a living. They are a very human way of making life more bearable. Practicing an art, no matter how well or badly, is a way to make your soul grow, for heaven's sake. Sing in the shower. Dance to the radio. Tell stories. Write a poem to a friend, even a lousy poem. Do it as well as you possible can. You will get an enormous reward. You will have created something.
>
> —Kurt Vonnegut, *A Man Without a Country*

Your dragons are going nowhere. Paint them. Write about them. Sew them and fold them and mix them and sculpt them and sing them and light them on fire. Dragons love fire. Fire is home. Fire is light. Heat is good. Heat makes strength. This is art.

I will create something

Decide it, if it suits you.

I will build something

I will make a story
A space
A room
A quilt
A thank-you
A letter
A song
A scream
I will put this somewhere.

We are healed of a suffering only by experiencing it to the full.

—Marcel Proust, *La Fugitive*

Wipe your eyes.

There will be plenty of pub bathrooms. You won't always collapse. All the anniversaries of your baby's birth or death will be loaded, but sometimes, the day will just pass. An anniversary can be creative and generative. It can make you feel ambivalent or connected. What feels perfect one year—lighting an origami boat on fire and watching it float away and burn—might strike you as trite and unnecessary the next year. Sometimes, you will have a long chat with death. You will part and say *See you next year* or *See you next week.* Other times, you'll turn away in a huff or hide from it under your bed, watching as death's feet enter your room and stand there a minute. You'll peer out and see death scratching its head, wondering where you are. Death will amble off, not holding it against you. It will be back.

These days, these annual signposts, will change as your pain changes. You will grow out of some rituals and adopt others. You will invite people into your remembrance some years and insist on total solitude in other years.

You will have no clue what to do. And you'll know exactly.

Chronic means that it will be permanent but perhaps not constant.

—Alice Munro, *The Love of a Good Woman*

CHAPTER NINE

Dog Paddling in #Truth

How to be accountable and evolve when a good chunk of
your soul feels encased in concrete. The faraway places your
mind must go, being among the grieving.

NOTES FOR THIS chapter: the art, comedy—if there is
any—and science of being among the misfortunate. A
disgusting and beloved chew toy of fragile rationalizations and
emotional Bermuda Triangles, and you are the dog. I am the
dog. At what point do we abandon this active, wide-awake grief?
At what point does it abandon us? Can we gnaw forever upon
something that will only stink more with every slobby bite and
squeak? When does self-awareness—"standing in my truth"
blah, blah—morph into me being *Winnie the Pooh*'s Eeyore?
At what point does the scale tip over into unhealthy territory?
What's so bad about Eeyore, anyway? Eeyore is splendid. Eeyore
is the art.

The comedy of grief, for me, is in graduating from Eeyore
to Bugs Bunny, outwitting the hapless coyotes who once made
me feel small. Spring-loading trip lines and flipping the tracks
of Wild West freight trains and loading cannons full of molas-
ses. Bugs always wins, and with style. Someone would unleash
another drive-by assault, and I would imagine throwing a wet
fish at her face. A catapult of wet fish, a thousand.

There's a strange and wonderful rush you get from sitting

with someone who not only shares dark feelings, but dark laughter. Tell me your worst. I'll tell you mine.

Holy shit. You're joking. That's horrible! And you still have to do Christmas?

By the end of it, our mutual outrage makes us smile.

The science of grief is a constant measurement: Am I okay? *Yes. For now.* Or *No, but maybe I will be tomorrow.* Or *Maybe not. I need to introduce a new element.* I chart my emotional temperature, watch lines rising and falling. I note patterns. From a distance I see a spectrum, long-view trends despite occasional peaks and valleys. I learn.

Whether you share it or not, all this reckoning will occupy much of your mind for a long time. And while you might know   fiercely, I hope—that you are normal, you might not know how you are doing. *Am I thinking too much? How can I not think? It's like telling someone who's anxious to relax. I am not capable of not thinking. Especially with so much to think about.* It's not like anyone chooses to fixate, like some people live and breathe politics or baseball stats. A dragon moved into your body, set up camp, and started breathing fire. You feel it every minute of every day. You have no choice but to make peace with it, pay attention, tame it, negotiate some ground rules. Doing so requires an affinity for all that reckoning comprises: feeling, remembering, dreams, nightmares.

> The ouroboros is an ancient symbol depicting a serpent or dragon eating its own tail. Originating in Ancient Egyptian iconography, the ouroboros . . . is often taken to symbolize introspection, the eternal return or cyclicality, especially in the sense of something constantly re-creating itself. It also represents the infinite cycle of nature's endless creation and destruction, life and death.
>
> —Wikipedia

In the age-old image of the Ouroboros lies the thought of devouring oneself and turning oneself into a circulatory process. . . . The Ouroboros is a dramatic symbol for the integration and assimilation of the opposite, i.e., of the shadow. This feedback process is at the same time a symbol of immortality, since it is said of the Ouroboros that he slays himself and brings himself to life, fertilizes himself and gives birth to himself.

—Carl Jung, *The Collected Works of C. G. Jung*

To integrate and assimilate the opposite—the shadow—is the work you are doing right now. Relief in pain, pain in relief. Round and round and round.

You are eating your tail.

You should stop that.

That is not good for you.

This is what they said to me, people who weren't into Jung.

That is disgusting.

But I am whole, I said. See? Wholeness. This is what it looks like to integrate.

That is disgusting.

I am renewing myself.

That is disgusting.

I am renewing myself.

. . . .

For years, I hid from babies. I'd stand ten feet back until I "forgot something in the car" or "had to do the dishes." I couldn't help it. I don't know why. The only explanation comes in the form of the one word that pops into my head: *unreconciled.*

But a while back, there was a kid in a front yard in Calgary. His mom, not privy to my nerves, said *I need to do a thing for a minute, can you . . .* and then he was in my arms and she was elsewhere.

Uhh.

He could have been mine. You know those babies, the ones who look at you all still and goggle-eyed and their proportions are familiar and they could have been yours? I looked over my shoulder. I could see her in the kitchen. I put my nose to the top of his head for a sniff.

Ggrrrmph.

I felt a string of drool ooze down across one knuckle, then another.

Raaaaaaagh.

I didn't know I'd been evading them—all of them—until that moment, when I realized I finally wasn't. I took him outside, flipping him to face outward with a hand wrapped around one thigh so one leg dangled. We sat on a porch swing with the back of his head flopped on my chest, the pudge of his legs splayed out on my lap. I felt the sun, his spitty chin, his clean scent. I remembered it's nice, when you have a baby on your person— any baby—to look at things and talk about the things you see. *A ladybug! Clouds in the sky today. Green grass! I hear a mower.* You chitchat. We rocked a little, one of his fists smushed into his mouth. Then realizations, like flashcards:

I am finished.

I'd be finished even if I didn't want to be finished.

I don't not want to be finished.

Even if I wanted to not be finished, I'm old. I'm separated. Come apart. I'm leathery. People who have b-b-babies are married and fifteen years younger than me.

I have an exploding uterus.

I don't want another kid anyway.

. . .

I like this one, though.

Things got really quiet. Just me and his little heft, his sticky neck. And I didn't run away.

Ggrrrmphaaaf.

He had a nice smell, and I liked it. My chew toy of fragile rationalizations and emotional Bermuda Triangles took a hit.

. . . .

People said *You're so strong* as if I'd been granted a moment to choose pluckiness and had chosen right, like Little Orphan Annie stamping on Miss Hannigan's foot. After your very small baby dies in your arms, to exist at all is seen by others as admirable rebellion. But it's not. When doctors say *Follow me,* you follow. When they say *Do this,* you do. The system sweeps you up, propelling you and cutting you loose at the same time. Holding your child's death certificate in your hands, you are more zombie than plucky. You don't feel strong at all. But somehow, you still exist, and so people will marvel, and every *You're so strong* reminds you, again, of the short straw you pulled. The platitude giver throws salt over a shoulder, having dodged the need to be the courageous-in-grief protagonist themselves, at least for the time being. Saying *Thank you* or *I'm trying* or nothing at all—just nodding in receipt—is weird, isn't it. It just is.

What is strong, anyway?

1. Brawny, strapping, sturdy, burly, robust, convincing.
2. Able to withstand great force or pressure. Secure, indestructible, fortified, protected, impregnable, well-defended.
3. The fastest way to weakness.

If you buy into the common illusion of strength, you're erecting a false front of indestructability. This is what makes the world sick. To be convincing wastes energy. To be impregnable is to self-isolate. To be robust is to be static, closed to growth. Strength is a pressure cooker. Strength is deodorant on gangrene. To be strong is to be stiff, and to be stiff is to be unpliable. Strength cracks.

Antonym: vulnerable. Be open and bendy, like fresh growth on a tree. Be malleable and tender, with proficiency in movement. This way, you are able to sit with all that's insecure, easily destroyed, unfortified, unprotected, and porous. You are unthreatenable because when you're not afraid of uncertainty, you've got nothing to protect. And when you've got nothing to protect—your image, illusions, defenses—you are supple. This is my preferred strength. Tolerance. How ice cream melts, still delicious. How a field turns into a pond and back again.

· · · · · · · ·

The first dead body I had ever seen or touched was the dead body of my son. And so I know: anything can happen. Nothing can be done about it. I will live the rest of my life in a state of constant fear.

Or

The first dead body I had ever seen or touched was the dead body of my son. And so I know: anything can happen. Nothing can be done about it. I will live the rest of my life in a state of constant release.

· · · · · · · ·

They say if your brain registers an imminent car crash, fight the urge to tense every muscle in your body. Being rigid is how we exacerbate our own injury. Go limp.

Could I? It's not what my body would want to do. My body would want to clench every tooth, grip, joint, and sinew, as though by hanging on to itself it might combat the force of impact. But it can't. The inertia that would crumple a car is a thousand times more powerful than me. If I go limp, there's a chance I might knock around inside disaster with a fraction more fluidity. Gone limp, I might break a little less.

· · · · · · · ·

I love a thesaurus. I love the confirmations of language. Grief Boggle! Mix and match:

TO GIVE UP

abandon | forfeit | surrender | free | relinquish | resign | release | part with | forgive | desist

TENSION

stress | hostility | friction | anxiety | nervousness | strife | pressure | conflict | unrest | aggravation | trepidation | strain | resistance | convulsion

TRY

attempt | seek | examine | endeavor | prove | taste | test | sample | practice | aim | intend | push | get | take | give | find | decide | use

GIVING UP

abandon | forfeit | surrender | freedom | relinquish | resign | release | part with | forgiveness | desist

. . . .

Nobody ever says the word *forbearance* anymore. The Victorians are long gone. But I needed something less ambivalent than release, more sacred than a shrug. Forbearance. Is that it?

Delay enforcing rights, claims, or privileges; refrain from action; a good-natured tolerance of delay or incompetence.

My right and claim to not ever witness a dead son, for a start.

Also under *forbearance*: Fail. Withhold action. Pause. Abstain. Seek magnanimity, graciousness, prudence, kindness, compassion. Be liberal and lenient with what sometimes simply just is. Diligently practice humility and generosity. See the curious Latin underpinnings that link mercy and loving-kindness to apathy, which is to waive resistance in favor of forgiveness.

Release.

Sometimes, having held my dead son, I am afraid. I know

anything can happen. I drift into an uneasy sleep as my brain off-gasses visions of deep water, of flailing arms and a small, scruffy head. I can't swim fast enough. I never can.

Shhh

The fear is a thing, a noun, an occupant. It enters my space and knocks everything over, filling my thoughts with catastrophe.

What if what if what if?

It happened before.

Shhh. To give up tension, try giving up on tension.

> Water does not resist. Water flows. When you plunge your hand into it, all you feel is a caress. Water is not a solid wall, it will not stop you. But water always goes where it wants to go, and nothing in the end can stand against it. Water is patient. Dripping water wears away a stone. Remember that, my child. Remember you are half water. If you can't go through an obstacle, go around it. Water does.
>
> —Margaret Atwood, *The Penelopiad*

Flow gently around and beyond people who tell you to quit eating your own tail. There is no need to try. Just flow, and keep flowing.

> In struggling against anguish one never produces serenity; the struggle against anguish only produces new forms of anguish.
>
> —Simone Weil, letter to André Weil

Your infinite relationship with your missing baby is your own private wholeness. You may let some select people into it for an afternoon or a lifetime. You may keep it to yourself. Leave other peoples' struggles with your struggles outside.

What the Italians so prettily call *stamina*. The vigor, the fire, that enables you to love and create. When you've lost that, you've lost everything.

—Simone de Beauvoir, *The Woman Destroyed*

Vulnerability—to continue loving and creating in the face of loss—is the only real strength. When you fall prey to people who make you feel like vulnerability is weakness, you fall. Do not lose your inner wick, the green strand of persistent aliveness seen in a cut twig that would otherwise, from the outside, appear to be brittle and dead. Tend to your conversations with nature, spirit, and baby. This is your stamina. Cultivate the fortitude to be still in this place. Be brawny, sturdy, and robust in your care of yourself. Withstand great force by making your inner relationships and imagination impregnable and well-defended.

What does your strength look like? Do you look people in the eye? Do you avoid going out? Do you talk at length whenever someone asks you how you're doing? Do you say almost nothing? Have you lashed out *I am fine, leave me alone,* or *I am not fine, why are you leaving me alone?* Do you nurse a growing heap of resentments and broken trusts? Are you buckling under their weight? Are you protecting someone from you? Are you protecting yourself from someone?

Any yes is a form of strength. You are strong enough to look after yourself like you would look after your baby. Strong enough to be clear about what you need in the moment you need it, regardless of expectations. Strong enough to either face the day, soldiering, or give it to grief, bleed clean for a few hours. The point is to define this state for yourself. It is not how you behave or what you do or the way you define healing that defines strong. It is how you safeguard your right to your instincts. Some of us will chatter uncontrollably for a year or two or more. Others will go silent. When I say *Stay wick* and *Stay open*, I'm not saying *Be like me*. That would make no sense. I am a dog's breakfast, a big mess, like you are, though your big mess will be yours. When I say *Stay wick* and *Stay open*, I mean flow gently around anyone who thinks you're doing it wrong no matter how you're doing it. Except water is not gentle. Water is determined, intentional, softly inexorable. There's nothing more pliable and more uncompromising than water.

Strong is strong like water.

· · · · · · · ·

The other day I saw a book about grief with one of those jaunty titles. Something about healing tears. It was for young widows and widowers, and it looked sweet and irreverent.

> IRREVERENT: lacking in proper respect or seriousness. Blasphemous, impious, profane, sacrilegious.

It had daisies on the cover. I flipped it open. The gist of what I saw was about how anger is toxic, a horrible thing to carry around. *You are going to be angry, but you've got to move past it or else it'll fester. Nobody wants to be an Angry Person.*

Fair enough, though the me of eight or nine years ago scowled. I looked at the cover again. Daisies. I scanned a bit more. It was a perfectly chilled glass of white wine on a beautiful fresh day. I had wandered into someone else's house of grief, one distinct from mine. Why did it make me feel so out of sorts? I wondered if I was—or am—too angry. And in love with the anger, my chew toy. Though there's plenty of other good things I'm in love with too, I still nose the anger around now and then. Have a bite. Make it squeak.

I thought about the word *irreverent*. Is she irreverent for finding good cheer and presentability despite sadness? Or am I irreverent for endorsing sadness in a world that oppresses the grieving by demanding good cheer and presentability?

Next to me, that book is wearing a head scarf tied like a 1950s pinup. She wears red lipstick and answers the door well. Is she better at this than I am? Did she #LetGo of her anger and learn how to tie a head scarf like a 1950s pinup? Am I cynical? Were those people who insisted I was doing it wrong right about me? Or was I right about me? If I claim my anger as an important heat, do I cattle brand myself with it? Am I afraid of liking that book because it'll tell me to put down this red-hot stick?

By turning toward grief, at least for a while, we turn away from proper respect and seriousness. We are irreverent. Topless feminists at a march in 1964. Topless feminists at a march in 2016. Antiestablishment righteousness can only be loud and proud. The self cannot be claimed politely, and the same goes for a future beyond pain.

After the death of someone we love, we counter a get-over-it world with storytelling, remembrance, and good, clean, complicated healing. It's radical to say anything other than *Fine* when someone asks you how you're doing. So be radical. And when you feel like it, seek out cheer and try on presentability. Buy books with daisies on the cover. It's good practice. But make space, too, if you feel like it, for profane rage—the kind of overwhelming bitterness that's sacrilegious to anyone who passive-aggressively gives you a book about the power of positivity. Profane rage is irreverent, too. Don't resist or fear it. It won't stick to you like ticks or lice or a bad stink. Its origins are worth talking about. You'll be more compassionate, alive, and healthy for having given it a voice. You'll grow a deeper appreciation and sensitivity to things suddenly feeling okay. You'll get there faster, and laugh louder when you do. Ask any punk.

. . . .

Despair comes in two flavors. Rage lights the flaming bags of dog shit; self-pity is the crippling woe. Both are fed by a totally normal, temporary blindness to relativity.

Standing there peering through the window of someone else's stress, you might think—against your conscience, your intellect, and your will—*What a lightweight. This person thinks they've got it bad, but they don't know bad. They haven't had a baby die. I am Medusa. Not you.*

Someone else, at some point, will peer through your window: *What a lightweight. This person thinks they've got it bad, but they don't know bad. They haven't <insert impressively horrific event here>.*

Your knee-jerk and their knee-jerk are the jerks of early trauma. It doesn't mean you're self-absorbed. It doesn't mean you're going to spend the rest of your life competing in the Pain Olympics. It means you're stuck, for a while, in the dreadful and circular gauntlet of *Why Me?* It means you're still processing. And that's alright. It is your weep, your wail, your dragon breath. It is the comforting taste of your own tail. With time, it will soften and fade along with the most immediate pain—softer, softer again until empathy returns.

Every now and then, someone sends kind but qualified words: *I've had (miscarriage / sickness / infertility / loss of spouse / loss of parent) and it was nothing compared to what you went through, but it broke my heart, and I'm sorry your heart was broken too.*

We saunter through life like *Doo de doo* and *La di dah* until an explosion blows the blinders off our eyes—an embryo slips, an eleven-year-old lies in an induced coma, a fearsome diagnosis emerges from a tidy doctor's office—and we realize we've been sauntering along the edge of a precipice all along. Only then can we see it, so terrified we can hardly move one foot in front of the other. Backs pressed against the wall, the one misstep that will send us to our doom plays over and over again in our heads. The pathway might narrow until our toes hang off the edge. We are paralyzed.

We lose the blinders eventually, one way or another, a lonely shock no matter what form it takes. All we can do is be good company to one another, marking the most ancient of conditions: birth, love, longing, loss. Heartbreak, no matter its source, is the most universal tax on the human experience. We might as well share in the payment of it.

. . . .

Medusa, on her own, is the void. A room full of Medusas is afternoon tea. Snakes intertwine. The milk is warm and so is the honey. Somebody new stumbles in with her head a tangled, hissing mess. *What kind of a monster am I?* she wails. *How did this happen to me?* We give her a hot mug and a soft place to sit.

I've still got my snakes, but me-as-Medusa looks more like a 1970s iron-on T-shirt than a nightmare. She's cool with me and I'm cool with her. She keeps it tucked in, mostly. There are dandelions growing in Chernobyl.

We are the mothers and fathers of spirits. We are walking proof of two worlds touching. My baby and yours, breathing for a time or not, were grown open, born open, and left open, still connected to their ancient selves. I'd like to think they knew just where to go, what happens next, and why they were here. Why not?

Once the soft machine of skin and bone is gone, what's left? Not our plot twists. Not all that was done and undone. Take away all that and we are infinitely renewing energy, more than the sum of our experiences. More than snakes. But since we've got them, we will find each other in a crowd.

. . . .

We sit outside by the creek. Josh and Kari tell me about someone who told them once, trying to normalize grief, that the aftershocks of loss never get better. We decide that's not true at all. We remember how it felt when it was new. And we know how it feels now. They say Liam's name, and I say Margot's name, and we all feel warm.

They ask how things are, being on my own. I tell them about years of one hurt being upended by another, about how divorce pain is not more substantial but much meaner than death pain. We talk about the mystery of little reprieves, and I tell them about the kids and me and our getaways: how the three of us get greasy brown bags of french fries from Bud the Spud's truck and check into the fancy hotel and jump on the beds and dance around to radio pop and put bath bombs in hot water with a *ploosh*, and they sit three feet deep in steamy bubbles and splash gets everywhere, and then we climb into a crisp white bed and read *Tweety & Sylvester* with Chupa Chup suckers. Josh knows wood and asks me questions about my butcher block. We talk about skiing and California. Mussels are all they've got up the street, so I make them with salted herbs and lemon and beer, and we eat and talk while the fire burns high into the tree canopy, and they say *Liam*, and I say *Margot*, and together we decide being open is the way to better.

CHAPTER TEN

An Imagination Sandwich with Religious Wonder Bread Whether You Ordered It or Not

In loss, spiritual comeuppance camps out on your front lawn
no matter what your inherited or practiced worldview.

B ABIES ARE NOT born of virgins, for god's sake, as though the only guarantee of holy purity is to never pass through the tainted channel of a Jezebel. Babies are born from the tainted channels of Jezebels! Angels sing on earth! Except the angels do not sing "Hosanna to the Son of David," or "O Magnum Mysterium." Real angels sing the theme song to *Lego Ninjago: Masters of Spinjitzu.*

My niece Molly giggles. Every time she does—which is a lot— baby blue and lemon-scented bubbles float into the air and then *pop!* burst glitter and sparkles all around. She is a little girl, a big girl. She reads the voice of every character with inflection. She likes it when adults are ridiculous, forgetting a dog says *woof* and not *meow.* She rides her bike, rainbow beads clacking on the wheels, and baby blue and lemon-scented bubbles full of glitter and sparkles trail along behind her.

I like to think Jesus would object to the OxiClean bleaching of his mother. I like to think while pressing R2-D2 into Luke Sky-walker's X-Wing Fighter with Power Functions, he'd crack the thing down the middle and say *Damn.* And Molly would look up and say *Hey, Jesus. That's just what Lego does. Have a cookie.*

Perfection bores me. I don't trust it. If it didn't have such tragic consequences on the world, the lie/myth/fetishization of female purity (or lack of it) would be a real eye roller of a joke. Baby blue and lemon-scented glitter bubbles are what's holy, and they begin with lust and arrive with an imperfect splash. I want a host of gods, and I want none of them whitewashed. I want one of them to be in charge of bubbles. I want them to be socialists, to look after each other and share accountability and resources fairly. I want a community of magicians to craft the world—all we see of it and all we don't—and I want them to spring forth from a godmother who counts down from ten, loudly, until the Bionicles get picked up, or else.

When I asked Molly if she always laughs like that, she laughed like that. Then she looked at me, puzzled, like there's no line distinguishing a good laugh from this morning or yesterday or tomorrow. Deep inside, her soul shook its head. *That poor grown-up, forgetting. Don't you ever lose it, Miss Molly,* her soul whispered, hoping she would hear. And I agree. Don't let the years pop your bubbles. Your bubbles are your purity, dear sweet lovely little big girl. Your bubbles make you holy. Insist upon them.

. . . .

We were Anglicans. My parents and my brother and I lived in England for a year, in Newcastle upon Tyne, when I was four years old. I had a Geordie accent and a swing in the yard. We spent the summer on a canal boat in Scotland. I almost saw the Loch Ness Monster from the ruins of a castle window. Almost. My brother and I worked the locks, and we ran alongside the water on ancient footpaths, my rubber boots kicking morning dew into the air like diamond bursts.

British cathedrals called to my mom and dad because all of Britain did. It was where our families came from. There is a pub in Cambridge with my grandfather's RAF unit and name gouged into the beams with someone's pocket knife. Choral singing made all the hair on my arms stand up, and my dad sang, so my brother and I did too, and our Sundays were high-necked white ruffs and long gowns, descants and candles. It's proper and good to get dressed up and to go and sing under a carved ceiling forty feet high, with sunshine streaming in through stained glass windows. You see people, and you have a nice tea, and you sing.

I had to go to Sunday school and be confirmed. It wasn't singing. It was boring. I asked my mom once, "The Sunday school teacher says God Is Everywhere. Is he in my milk? If I pour him on my cereal will he be mad? Does he see me when I pee? Ha ha!"

"For goodness sake, I don't know," she replied, smiling from behind her sewing machine. And that was the sum total, outside of choir practice, of my religious indoctrination. Or of any moral imperative, come to think of it, other than *Do unto others as you would have others do unto you.* My parents never explicitly told me not to smoke, make out with boys, drink, or swear. I didn't, in any case, because I was pretty green and stayed that way until it was well beyond the safe point to not be green. But the point is they trusted me. My parents' only absolute rules for my brother and me were what really matters:

Never litter. Leave places better than how you found them.

Never say shut up. *And never use the word* hate. *Not for anything. They are the two rudest things you can ever let out of your mouth. It is never justified, no matter how upset you are. I don't care who else says it. We do not.*

I will not have either of you leave this house without knowing how to make pastry and mayonnaise and birthday cakes from scratch.

Don't make your family worry. Take care of yourself.

Be nice. Leave people feeling better than how you found them.

. . . .

Sorry . . . a faceless person hissed, trolling my friend's online campaign against a constitutional amendment to ban gay marriage in Arizona. *Marriage is a special and sacred covenant designed by God to be between a MAN and a WOMAN!*

If energy and atoms recycle, then we've all had marginalized incarnations. Each of us has been born and reborn, with ill-timed turns at being poor, female, Protestant, black, Jewish, Irish, Ojibwe, or gay. In all of those states we were a living, breathing expression of renewal, just as we were. In all of those states we have been denied. Too many of us forget to remember, when we're most recently born into local privilege: the Other could easily be you.

A baby dribbles cereal for the first time, and we think *Oh! Look at you go. Good girl!* and she is a hairline closer to making her own way in the world. We are proud, so proud. Then she crawls like greased lightning. Then she Weeble-wobble walks. Then before we know it she's got the keys to the car, and we hear the voice of our parents from our own mouths: *It's not you I'm worried about. It's all the other drivers*, and we won't sleep a wink that night until she is safe in her bed.

Parenthood is one long letting go. Our children grow up, up and away, and they need us less and less, and there's no use resisting it. But the collective of human beings doesn't grow up, up and away. As we grow, fumbling to feel around the edges of this world we've been given, those edges close in. The world gets smaller and smaller still thanks to technology. We can video-conference with Indonesia. Borders are vanishing. There are planes and there is high-speed rail and we've never been so mobile, so empowered to seek and explore. Human beings are squashing together. There's no longer the space to remain cloistered in like-minded tribes. We bump and jostle, forced by sheer proximity to look at each other—really look—and exist among the unfamiliar sights and sounds of others.

In this cacophony there are now only two breeds of human: those whose judgments and self-righteousness make them wish for a fantasy yesterdayland, backward in time to when what felt different was policed and rejected:

Quit shoving! You stink.

I'm better than you.

Shut up. Move over.

He stepped on my foot! Somebody do something.

This is unbearable. This is wrong.

You are unwelcome.

This has to stop.

And there are those who shrug:

> I suppose, ten million years from now, we'll all be just alike
>> Same color, same kind, working together
>> And maybe we'll have all of the fascists out of the way
> by then.
>> —Woody Guthrie, "She Came Along to Me"

Social progress is as certain as a current in a bottleneck. To push against it is masochistic and misguided, inevitable failure proven time and time again. Granting more people respect, self-determination, and agency over their own happiness is the shrug that might save the world. Only when we quit spending so much energy excluding one another can we redelegate. Only then can we begin the work of solving actual problems.

Loss makes compassion by connecting us to the human experience. With pain, with almost unbearable hurt. But nonetheless, we are connected. We are awake. First, we harden up—so bitter, so upset—but then we soften, softer, softer, and softer still until we truly understand why we are here. To share love. To share understanding. None of us have the time for anything less.

Dave is a rabbi and bereaved dad. He and his wife Gal learned in the middle of her pregnancy their baby Tikva might not survive for long beyond her birth. He wrote:

> *I always suspected that deep down inside, the person yammering on about unconditional love was really trying to set himself up to get a piece of ass. Nothing wrong with that, but don't kid yourself about unconditional love. Until you've lived it, you can't know it. And the separation between those who can grasp the concept and those who have held the feeling is a yawning chasm that nothing but experience can bridge. Until you love your child without ever knowing whether or not you'll ever get to hold her, you don't know unconditional love. Until your love for your child is greater than your need for her to live even one more day with anything less than the dignity she deserves, you don't know unconditional love.*

To that particular faceless religious conservative: Imagine a crystal ball trained on the future of the child you hold in your arms. The child with the succulent, cheesy neck, the chubby folds. The child who woke up twice last night in hot tears and needed you, just you. What if the crystal ball told you she's gay? When she grows up she'll live far away, but she'll be home every summer and for Christmas with her wife. They want kids, a couple of kayaks, a lakeside cottage. She's going to be happy and smart and an engineer and gay. Does that change anything?

If the crystal ball told you the baby in your arms would die, you'd beg and plead *Just keep her safe and whole. I will cheer her on forever no matter what.* As you should.

Everybody started out as somebody's baby. People who live and love and think differently. People we feel are our aesthetic, spiritual, or cultural opposite. People who are struggling, or who carry pain you can't see. Give them love regardless of how they align (or don't align) with you. Let them show you who they are on their terms, not yours. Give them unconditional hospitality, and mean it. Don't think it's enough to insist you only hate the sin and not the sinner. Try not hating anything that is, respectfully, none of your business. Ask them how they're doing and mean it. It's incredible how quickly we forget how rare that is. Look at every person and think *There goes somebody's baby. Could have been mine.*

Then go find a mirror and extend the same to what you see.

R.E.M. might have written the next holy book. One page. Two words. Every doctrine and every mandate of compassion and care should begin and end here.

Everybody hurts.

. . . .

You have your way. I have my way. As for the right way, the correct way, and the only way, it does not exist.

—FRIEDRICH NIETZSCHE, *Thus Spoke Zarathustra*

In loss, spiritual comeuppance camps out on your front lawn no matter what your inherited or practiced worldview. Some of us subscribe to God with a capital *G*. Or the universe. Or Allah or Buddha or Shakti or Gitche Manitou, the "Great Mystery" of the Anishinaabe. No matter which particular divine prophet or entity is yours, loss is a galvanization: is the Great Mystery a senselessly abandoning prick? Delusion incarnate? Gandalf the White sitting on a cotton ball throne, the Bible in one hand and a slate of the Ten Commandments in the other, hurricanes and AIDS and salvation shooting out from the tips of his fingers from beyond the pearly gates of so many punch lines? Or, is it nature's random dust and growth? The wind, the waves, the monarch butterflies. Then there's ghosts and angels and spirits and souls and energy and chi and serendipity and karma. Semantics. We cannot follow the dead.

The great cruelty of outliving children is that mothers and fathers are baptized into parenthood with the instinct to follow with mushy carrot, with a tug on slipping-off socks and the bumpering of a sharp-cornered world. Following is our assumed right and rite of passage. We follow with every last inch of gut and marrow, compelled by her round belly's sweet rise and fall and by the smudges of milk stuck in the creases of her neck.

The bereaved are compelled just the same by phantoms. But how can we be caregivers, the hallmark task of parents, when they are gone? How do we mind them when we can't follow them?

The particular loss of this particular love makes us dumb as june bugs. We rattle and hum against a light we'll never bathe in, never reach. We can see it, almost touch it, but screens and closed windows keep us out. *Bash. Bam. Crack. Follow. Follow. Follow. Bash. Bam. Crack.* We are sticky and crunchy. We chase people inside. To make us go away, they say things about how the screens and the glass are all a part of God's Plan.

No
No
No
No
No
Bash
Bam
Crack

. . . .

Evan said, "What's that?"

"That's my notebook," I replied.

I had gone for a three-day meditation retreat at the Shambhala Centre in Halifax, a toe dip into an interesting pool when the Rinpoche happened to be in town. Kind of neat. Something to try. It was quiet, and it was nice.

"I want to see," he said. "I want to know what happened today."

He tossed *Flat Stanley* and climbed up on the big bed. Ben scrambled up too. One boy here and one boy there and me in the middle and one small lamp.

"Well, sweetness, there was a man from Tibet, and there were scary people, and he had to run away through the mountains, and he had a son, and his son had interesting things to say. He came into the room wearing bright orange and bright yellow robes and everybody bowed. And he sat up high and he talked and he talked, and I was so tired by then because I'd been sitting there like a sardine in a can for two and a half days, and I could hardly listen but I heard, I think."

He thought about that. "Why?"

I told him what the man in orange and yellow robes said, in the same words: "Twenty-five hundred years ago, they discovered The Most Boring Thing Ever. They meditated to contextualize their existence. And it was boring. And they said 'Hey! This is great!'"

I told him how everybody laughed and the room got warm.

"You cannot nullify fear," the Tibetan man had said. "Soft elements are essential. Put human nature in a state of photosynthesis and goodness will arise. Sit with small confidences. To sit is to be regal."

Evan looked over my shoulder, scanning pages of fragments and doodles.

"The mind is a horse," he read aloud, struggling a little with my loopy scrawl. And he thought for a bit. "What's that mean?"

"What do you think?" I asked him. He thought a bit more.

"Maybe . . ." he ran his hand back and forth over the paper. "A horse is really strong, but it needs somebody to make sure it doesn't knock everything over."

After, in the dark: "Mommy. That would be good for my temper."

· · · · · · · ·

On a long, winding descent I would gear up, flying past farms and cattle to arrive at the office feeling rosy and substantial. There's no better feeling than to move your body around on a bike.

A manhole marked the halfway point of a long hill. For a year's worth of days it was my ritual to ride over its cover because it made a satisfying *kathunk-thunk*. One morning, the dark circle came up fast. At the last second I startled at the sudden voice of my grandmother, a cyclist who had died a few years back. Two urgent words, like a shout: *TURN NOW.*

I obeyed, swerving to miss the manhole by inches, looking down to prove myself paranoid as I passed. I was going as fast as the cars. It was uncovered and unmarked. The gaping hole would have swallowed the front end of my bike, pitching my head and neck into the edge of the asphalt at near-highway speed. Squeezing the brake levers hard I slowed, jumped off, and walked back with my legs shaking to gape at what might have been. I rode the rest of the way to work and called the municipal road crew, thoroughly rattled.

My grandmother's voice. The presence in the room the day Liam died. A sixth sense? Imagination? Do intense moments simply initiate a cerebral protocol, like that initiated at the split second of a car crash? A man tumbles violently inside a Toyota Corolla. A fuse in his brain blows. Later, waking up in hospital, he remembers nothing after reaching to change the radio station. Is that our physiological wiring, or some kind of cosmic benevolence? Was the breaking of my neck on the edge of a manhole—or me swerving around, and carrying on down the road—nothing more than a hiccup either way? Or did my grandmother wrestle her way through the divide, even for a flash, to warn me? Was Liam's life a hiccup? Was he an egg and a sperm that divided and divided again, was betrayed by his mother's placenta, and was born sick and died to be set loose in a lake, a handful of ash? Perhaps. Maybe he was never mine, fated, chosen. Maybe he was just an organic reaction, his conception as much of a "whoops" of nature as his injury and death. Is this glass half empty or half full? Should I cry? For which reason? Even as nothing more than ash, was Liam the stuff of stars?

If what happened to you and me was nothing more than biology, blind misfortune, or random chance, then there was no meaning to it. No divine entity let us down. We are part of the natural world, and the natural world is chaos. Loss is a happenstance. Some baby cells are still inside us, remaining, while others feed the roots of a maple or rest for a blink in the belly of a trout. Maybe that's accompaniment enough, as long as we pay attention to it.

· · · · · · · ·

For the Anishinaabe people, Gitche Manitou is the creator of all things and the giver of life. Sometimes, the word means the "Great Mystery," the fill-in-the-blank for all we can't account for with our eyes. But Gitche Manitou is not a being. Closer to the East Asian concept of *qi*—life force, energy flow—than that of a holy spirit, it refers to the interconnectedness of nature and life.

This force is also known as *prana* to the Hindus and Indians, *chi* in the Igbo religion, *pneuma* to the ancient Greeks, *mana* to the Hawaiians, and *lüng* to Tibetan Buddhists. Everything has its own manitou. Every plant, stone, organism, and even machine. Manitous do not exist in a hierarchy like gods or goddesses but are more like leaves on a tree, each distinct and individual but interacting with each other and the spirit of everything.

But my baby is gone, you might say. *I don't care what they said about energy in ancient Greece.*

There might be something useful waiting for you in ancient Greece.

A crow is beautiful. They're everywhere, but we don't tend to look. Silky, shiny black. Always with others. Fierce in feeding, fierce in protecting. Clever. Collectors. Little pirates, they are. But big. Imagine a crow perched on your hand. Doubly so for the raven, crow's big brother. For the Haida people, the raven's domain is tricks, transformation, and potent ingenuity. He is the deviant hero and survivor who created the Haida Gwaii—a glorious and sacred rainforest archipelago along British Columbia's northern coast—by releasing the sun from its box and igniting the stars and moon. All over the world and in every chapter of human life, scholars and artists have always been enamored of the raven's capacity to create by stealing, exchanging, and redistributing whatever catches his eye. It's a sacred power.

To the wonder and poetry of the natural world you might add a bearded prophet or a fat-bellied happy man in lotus position or an elephant deity with four arms full of useful things or any number of holy books. Throughout your lifelong practice of rationalizing loss, nothing will (or should) feel like the absolute truth. The only absolute truths can be found in puppies, cream cheese icing, and cold sprinklers on hot days. Everything else is bits and pieces. Proverbs, psalms, hymns, chants, recitations. Ghostly warnings and intuition. Temples and Quakers and monks. In the void of answers after loss, be a crow. Collect interesting things. A shoelace. An empty french fry bag. Blown-about Christmas tinsel. Tug on whatever spiritual fragment catches your eye, no matter its origin. Follow instinct more than dogma. This is your private survival.

In the aftermath of loss, our faith—or the philosophical, spiritual, and scientific tendrils we use to make sense of our human life—is often upended. A crow survives by borrowing from ancient Greece. We have been watching babies die since then and long before that, after all. Regardless of spiritual inheritance, we are parents first because we are animals first. You are drawn to care for a baby by its sweet scent. Your lineage compels you to rear offspring and mourn them, an impulse predating all religions by countless millennia. The love of a parent for its child is more adhesive and more ancient than all the gods, hardwired into us when we were Australopithecus, mere infants in our own evolution, long before the tenets of Jesus or Buddha or Muhammad or the Torah or anyone or anything else arrived on the scene. Regardless of what you believe, I share this impulse with you. We all do.

> Tikva's passing, on a feeling level, is exactly the depth of life I desire. I wouldn't have asked for the conditions in a million years, but the "why" of it isn't for me to answer.
> —David (Jewish)

> Perhaps V had his own thing to do, his own destiny, one which I could not—and maybe even should not—have prevented.
> —Rosepetal (Hindu)

I do not get to pick and choose what I experience. Just as I know bad things can strike out of the blue, I know it can't always be bad. The dice will come up with evens and odds—sometimes more evens, sometimes more odds.

—Natalie (atheist)

We held her for many hours after she died, and I would be lying if I said I didn't have it out with God during that time. I would be lying if I said I haven't had it out with Him every day since then. Yes, I believe. Absolutely. I don't know how to not believe. But I don't understand.

—Angie (Christian)

People outside lived their lives like nothing had happened. I thought the world had changed and everybody was in grief, but it was only us. My husband and I cried every day.

—Souad (Muslim)

You know how to behave to keep your tribal identity intact, if you feel you must, whether it's thanking your aunt for a My Little Angel embroidered pillow or showing up to temple when you know you'll get a call from your father if you don't. But to lose a baby is a questioning of everything you thought you knew. Explore, gently. Know that no matter your context or convictions, we all share bereavement. The Hindu sounds like the Jew who sounds like the Muslim who sounds like the atheist. We have more in common than not. We all leaked milk, and we all cried.

Take a peek in the house next door.

Your evangelism in an uproar, find a dog-eared copy of *The Soul of Rumi* in a secondhand shop. Open it and see a poem:

There is a window open
from my heart to yours.

From this window, like the moon
I keep sending news secretly.

Carry the writing of Jalāl ad-Dīn Muhammad Rūmī, a thirteenth-century Sufi mystic born in what is now Afghanistan, with you for months. Tattoo an open window onto a secret place only you can see.

Be a Jew who whispers to Ganesha, remover of obstacles and god of beginnings and patron of letters and learning: *Aum Vakratundaya Hum, Aum Vakratundaya Hum.* The Sanskrit is nice to say, soft in the mouth, like music, and nicer still when you find its meaning: "Delay no more, my Lord, in straightening the paths of the crooked mind."

Be a Hindu and note Viktor Frankl's words from the concentration camp in which he was held: "Everything can be taken from a man but one thing: the last of the human freedoms—to choose one's attitude in any given set of circumstances, to choose one's own way."

Be an atheist and adore something someone gave you from a Hebrew prayer book: "This is the vision of a great and noble life: to endure ambiguity and to make light shine through it; to stand fast in uncertainty; to prove capable of unlimited love and hope."

Be a Muslim and walk in the woods near the abbey where Buddhist nun Pema Chödrön wrote: "When we protect ourselves so we won't feel pain, that protection becomes like armor that imprisons the softness of the heart." Cape Breton maple leaves are a bit of yarn to add to your nest.

This is the survival of the crow. Steal, exchange, and repurpose regardless of what might be proper. Make shelter in the tree you've now found yourself in. Take what you need. Whatever catches your eye. Invent your heaven. I did. I will open a door. I will see a baby in a crib, and I will know it is him. My breasts will be full. I will hear him gurgling, chatting to himself, all clammy and goggle-eyed. *Halloooo, my baby love!* I will strip him down to his skin and lift him up, and he will arch his back, stretching and yawning. I will feed him. Then I will dress him fresh and wrap him in the mei tai, and we'll go say hello to the seagulls, his little head tucked in, my hand pat-pat-patting his rump, and this will be my afterlife.

Souls travel in packs, I've decided, and I have taken that for my nest too. They drift in and out of lives, drawn magnetically to one another time and time again across dimensions by what we think of as turns of fate. Driving in the car a long time ago, a four-year-old Evan piped up from the backseat: "A long time ago, Mommy, you and me were married in a white church."

"Really?" I smiled.

"Yes," he said. "We lived in a little house. We were married, a long time ago. You were my wife."

Maybe, when you're young, the door to all the answers is still open.

The Buddhists say life is suffering. Not joy interspersed with struggle but struggle interspersed with joy, a series of unwanted absences one after the other. This might sound miserable, but to know it is to be set free. The crow in me, satisfied, yanks on that prize and flies away.

Some people have missing babies. Some have missing parents, lovers, friends. What happened to you—to us—was an awful trauma. The effect of it brings us to the most fundamental human state of missing and to the painfully exquisite truth of loss. This should make us eternally conscious, but we're human. We don't thank our lungs for filling and emptying, our eyes for the sunrise, our kidneys for cleaning our blood. Our arteries and capillaries, ribbons passing along the current of our pulse. Our ears for giving us Prince's *Purple Rain*. Our skin for being in a constant state of renewal. Our muscles for keeping us upright, and the electrical panel of our brain for telling us when to blink, breathe, and run. Here we are, functioning. But to lack gratitude is as human as to suffer. We forget how inconstant life can be. We forget that with every fart and every sneeze, we are miraculous.

· · · · · · · ·

Your baby is not with us because she is in heaven.
  Jesus must have needed her more than you did.
  She is in a better place.

Oh, ye faithful: the moment you leave the room, the bereaved person you just informed of god's kind benevolence just flipped the bird at your back. Or they wanted to. And every other bereaved person in the world felt the energetic wobble of that middle finger and smiled.

On a broad scale, religion is semantics dividing the land masses of humanity to nobody's benefit. By the more urgent measures of shared interest and cooperation and community, semantics shouldn't matter as much as they do. Who cares how we privately reconcile the riddle of our humanity? Gods or ghosts or angels or prophets or spirits or souls or guardians or energy or chakra or gospel or chi or serendipity or karma or molecules, what does it matter? We are all made of the same primal stuff. We all know not to get in between a black bear and her cubs.

There are a hundred gods, a thousand. One for the caterpillar crossing a sidewalk; one for the daddy longlegs trapped in a bathtub puddle; one for every empty belly, tightrope walker, contracting uterus; one for every yellowfin tuna's gaping mouth; one for every screaming mackerel; one for every tin can.

From one angle, the gods fail every day. From another, the baby swallow's god tumbles alongside her from nest to ground and curls around her in the grass, dying with her, fulfilling everything.

CHAPTER ELEVEN

Nothingness and All There Is

We peek into the dust of nihilism and find warmth there.

S HE CAME INTO the room before the ceremony, as is the fashion these days, and he gasped and went to her, beaming, touching flowing fabric and lace, telling her how beautiful she was. And she was. Through the lens of my camera they shone, as brides and grooms do. They walked together down a grass aisle holding hands as a warm ocean breeze swept across them.

Even when we're young, before we can understand our own fragility and before statistics and cynicism rattle our certainty of the fairytale, we love a wedding. It is the brandishing of our collective best. It's the most sparkling, most affirming taunt we've got to throw—a *nonnie, nonnie, nah, nah* to our lack of guarantees. The universe smiles at our sass, grants us this day. We love the silhouette of a bride and a groom, archetypal proof of our efforts to navigate the unnavigable human condition. We like this vantage point. Its composition pleases us. We glow in their glow.

When I'm shooting a wedding, the first place I land is with the bride. She wears a robe or a plaid shirt. There are croissants and pink prosecco and the people around her fuss. *Eat something. You'll hardly get anything once this all starts.*

Someone new comes into the room and everyone squeals and hugs, and the cycle of fussing and adornment continues. The dress waits to costume her. Her friends lift it down like a slow-motion waltz. She disappears and comes out again in need of nimble hands for hooks and eyes, the last bit of her everyday self peeking out before the theater begins.

I spend the next ten hours lugging my kit, kicking off my shoes, hunting patches of light, being invisible. But what knocks me flat, every time—what I could never take lightly, no matter how wracked I was by the end of my own marriage—is the visceral responsibility of recording something that will never happen again. Not between these two particular people on this day, with these witnesses. These lovers who somehow found one another in the midst of all this noise and worry and fear.

The bride's name was Jen. She had cancer. I didn't know it the day I photographed their wedding. Not until after, when someone told me in a hushed voice. The same hushed voice told me the day she died, a few years later.

If we knew our exact number of days or years—the precise granting of how many weekend cuddles we would be given, with flannel sheets and comic books—we would squeeze goodness and gratitude out of every second. Every time someone dies, we think on this. Then we promptly forget it.

The glow, however fleeting, defines us just as much as all the rest.

· · · · · · · ·

I saw him at a Christmas party thrown by a friend. I gasped and stepped back before going to him and saying I was sorry, asking him how he was doing. To photograph a bride and groom is a deeply intimate thing. All day long, it's the three of you. Them and you. You see his hand shaking. You see his mother's hand shaking. You hear what her best friend whispers to her as they fasten an earring. I didn't know them, but I had shadowed them in a way nobody else had. And here he was, the groom without his bride. We stood by a table of salt cod pâté with bottles of beer. I knew him, having seen him at his wedding, but I didn't know him at all.

Our first words were of his wife and of Liam. He said *You've experienced loss, too, right?* Like when Luna Lovegood explains thestrals, the skeletal winged horses that only the grieving can see, to Harry Potter. I don't know how else to bridge the story from salt cod pâté to today other than to say we have been together ever since, which is how our being together began—as a bumble, as things are when you don't expect them. Her jar of organic cinnamon, with her handwriting on the label, is in my kitchen. For a long time I felt like an intruder, though by the time he met me, he had long ago come to terms with her prognosis. By the time he met me, he was ready to live again. Cancer will do that. Witnessing it exhausts you into life.

He tells me his dreams of her. Her parents and extended families, loving him as their adopted son and brother, are so kind to me it's made me cry in the car on the way home more than once or twice. This reckoning softens with time, but it's still there: if she hadn't gotten sick, I would still be on my own, insistent on being on my own while being wracked about being on my own. My husband would still be her husband. For a long time, it didn't feel right.

Jen's mother, Muriel, lost her little girl. I lost my little boy. We are both bereaved, though differently. Jen told her mother stories of her adventures in India. She graduated from art college while her mother beamed, her daughter's work hanging all through the house. She is gone, now. I am married to Muriel's son-in-law.

I'm sorry.

I can't help thinking it, an instinct.

I shouldn't be here. She should be.

· · · · · · · ·

From the moment we can know almost nothing, and from the moment that everything is limitless, what remains? Does emptiness actually not exist? What does exist in this apparent emptiness?

—GUY DE MAUPASSANT, *The Complete Works of Guy de Maupassant*

Me and you make a rude gesture at the emptiness. We are human! We are sentient. We know we will die. We rebel, refuse, and invent because we are frightened. Our defiance of the inevitable is the only thing that helps us sleep at night.

Cormac McCarthy and Albert Camus and Jean-Paul Sartre and all the world's romantics and vagrants alike wrestled and still wrestle, in scholarly auditoriums and dive bars alike, with why we exist. Are we born to watch clocks? Why bother hoping, performing? To what end? Why do we try, love, and die in this endlessly orgiastic, apparently purposeless combustion of body matter and dreams?

Competing glee clubs, religions aside:

The Nihilists (The world has no meaning, dumbass. None means none.)

The Existentialists (The world has no meaning, sweetheart. Hey. Since you're here, why not build something? Here's a hammer. . . . Neat! That thing you built has meaning.)

The Absurdists (The world has no meaning, silly. You're gonna turn yourself inside-out trying to fix that, though, aren't you? Because you're human. You can't help it. But you can't fix it. You're a sucker! I'm a sucker. Ha ha! WAIT. STOP. I smell something. I smell sticky toffee pudding. Sticky toffee pudding! Yay!)

If not reaching for some form of Heaven, humans undergo various intellectual contortions to try and answer unanswerable questions. Early explorers of emptiness took a shot at what they saw as the sheep-ism of religion, and they shot far and wide. They had to. Religion owned nation-states and populations en masse, at the expense of all else. *Wake up! Don't live well because God is alive. Live well because God is dead. God is dead!* That's the recoil: what looks like a bit of a circle jerk, really, of futility. "The point is there ain't no point," wrote McCarthy, inspiring as much of a league as the fundamentalists though with a different gospel: for some of them, the only way to be truly masterful is to never tolerate earnestness. But that's not all. Not at all.

> Everything that exists was born without reason and will die by chance. —Jean-Paul Sartre, *Nausea*

> If we believe in nothing, if nothing has any meaning and if we can affirm no values whatsoever, then everything is possible and nothing has any importance.
> —Albert Camus, *The Rebel*

It is true we don't learn how little mastery we have over our destinies until something goes terribly wrong. The crisis is in how cold Sartre's dark night feels and how unpromising and gray the morning dawn of Camus. But there's a useful seed in nothingness. Here it is: ease up on trying to figure out your loss of innocence, appetite, dignity, fertility, faith, fetuses, people you love. You won't. No matter what happens to us in our lives, it is unfigurable. Nothing and no one is deserving or undeserving. Everything is born. Everything dies. All is chaos. But then, consider the absurd: try again. Nothingness can live alongside tenacity and optimism. Turn over soil that lacks nutrients. It is a brittle crust. Nothing will grow in it. Be generative in a freshly tilled and damp plot. Pain is manure. Earnestness is sunshine. If nothing has any importance, than everything does. Even small things.

Everything is possible. That is Camus's dawn. We ascribe value and meaning to life when we produce it ourselves, free of doctrine. With his GOD IS DEAD, Nietzsche shook off the dogmatic yoke. Imagine determining what matters most with a clean slate and the common sense, do-unto-others morality of humanism. Rather than turning to a holy book for the answer of all answers, why not look to buttercream and vegetable gardens? This is why I'd share a bowl of sticky toffee pudding with Nietzsche. The nineteenth-century Prussian philosopher as seconded in Bob Marley's heaven-on-earth anthem "Get Up, Stand Up."

Nietzsche called the great emptiness our deepest opportunity for self-reflection. The moment you are strong enough to meet that emptiness—the cancer, the addiction, the miscarriage, the lost baby—you are strong enough to jump off the hamster wheel of thinking it through. *To move, stay put,* say the Buddhists. *To see, stop looking.* Don't imagine paradise in the sky. Make paradise in the kitchen.

. . . .

HOW CAN THIS NOT JUST BE SAD thinks a writer, jotting down notes for a book about grief. *Can I turn this around? Not just death death death. What's the takeaway? What's the point? To love, yeah. Of course. But more than that. How do we proceed?*

Justifiably alarmist environmentalism can have the unintended effect of making some people apathetic. We throw our hands up. An ice shelf the size of Maryland melting into the Bering Sea is too big a problem. We are too small. The resistance movement after Trump's election, which unfolds like a slow-motion train wreck as I write this book, seems to be doing the same. Mired in shock, individuals take what action they can. They want to keep moving forward in the interest of inclusion, decency, a free press, clean air and water. Not backward. They talk about it at supper parties. They retweet and share and call Congress. But they are dispirited. The world is too strange, and the strange is too big. How to proceed?

HOW CAN THIS NOT JUST BE OVERWHELMING
MEANINGLESS
SAD, etc.

The answer: I have hindsight. I can see around the corners you can't. Maybe not to specifics, but I can see your path turns, and you don't know what's beyond it. I can see enough to know you just have to keep trying. I saw Shawna as she stood alone at the Walk to Remember in Edmonton. I saw her unknown and unresolved. *I feel like Nothing, since this happened*, she wrote to me. But she was flushed with life no matter how she shrank from it in the absence of Ceili. I could see it in her, and I would see it in you. Everything is still there. I don't know what else to say about nothingness other than that.

· · · · · · · ·

The rusted-out shell of an old factory lay sleeping across the road. The paper in my bag said TEXTURE IN LANDSCAPE, one of several assignments toward my photography diploma. I was shooting with black-and-white film and loved the lines of the corrugated steel, the chasm and the darkness beyond its door. I raised the forty-year-old Pentax to my face. A long-legged dog appeared just then, emerging from the darkness like a submarine from the deep to sit regally, perfectly framed, in a shaft of light. It was the first time I remember hitting the shutter and feeling like I hadn't just taken a photograph, but captured a little wordless poem.

Throughout my twenties, I wandered Vancouver with pockets stuffed with rolls of film, encamped in darkrooms to paint with light. It's the only mathematics my brain has ever understood: the perfectly symbiotic interplay of aperture, shutter speed, ISO. It appeals to me as baking appeals to others in times of stress: no matter what is happening in the world, add powder or soda plus temperature and humidity and something sweet rises just so, indefatigably, no matter what. Like baking, photography is one of those lifelong pursuits. To capture moments and people and faces beautifully warms the room just the same as a hot oven.

· · · · · · · ·

My babies were a terrible sight. Liam in particular, in the first days after he was born. I was afraid of him, for him. His legs splayed open, his skin swollen and puffed, bright purple, every inch of him covered with intervention: blue tape, needles, IV, ventilator, bili lights. He was a cyborg, a specimen, a broken butterfly pinned to a board.

Having seen him, I knew I would have to figure out how to see him. His context knocked me off my feet. My fear was in the way of my love. To see the boy who might be—who might have been—his soft flesh, the baby underneath—I would have to work my way through his shocking circumstance. First, I picked up my camera almost in defense of his space, circling the intensive care unit like a caged animal. I knew what would happen if I allowed any camera other than mine close to Liam and Ben.

The incubator was a precisely controlled environment. The only way I could be inside with him, in his world, was with my lens. I shrank myself and curled up beside him, seeing him not through plastic but inside it. I saw toes and fingers, the clammy flush of heat, the softness at the nape of his neck. Every day, I pushed myself to go inside. Every day, a well-meaning nurse or relative might approach with a point-and-shoot and I would say

No snapshots. Well-meaning and blurry, well-meaning and sad, a reduction of him to his trauma. Someone else's pictures would compete with my narrative, in which he was more than that. His memory was mine to shape. This was how I loved him.

. . . .

Ben looks over my shoulder. I had been cleaning out an old hard drive, and we are scrolling. He sees Liam sucking on his fingers. He and his twin nose to nose, drifting in and out of sleep.

"I want to see that one! Is that him? Is that me? How did you know? How can you tell?"

Oh, darling. I could tell. I could see Liam's pain. Ben, love, you were already growing plump in small ways, your skin hanging off bird bones in folds like a Shar-Pei puppy but with a glow. Gram by gram you recovered in ordinary ways, extraordinarily. You fussed to get out of there and go home. I knew you from one another by every tiny wail of yours and by all of Liam's silence. Liam, my love . . . Liam had a pallor, a misshapenness, his fists curled up in distress. This is how I knew, sweetheart.

But I don't say that. I say, "I just knew." Ben smiles.

"Show me that one," he says, pointing at a thumbnail. I hesitate. It is from their first day or two. It makes me cry. There was no best effort to be made. He was an emergency. He was death. "Show me," says his identical brother, ten years later. "Whose foot is that?"

I double-click. "It's Liam, love."

"Oh . . ."

"I know."

"Why is it like that?"

"The first few days were very hard for Liam."

It is a photograph of the bottom of his heel. His ankle is wrapped in tape, holding lines in place. His skin shines taut over swollen blood, deep purple, and his foot is littered with pinpricks, only day two of his life but every second of it so far filled with distress.

"Why did they do that?" He is looking at the pinpricks.

"The doctors would take a little pinch of blood, and they would look at it under a microscope to see if it was okay."

"Was it okay?" He asked, hopefully.

Only in that moment, ten years later, I figured out why I fended off every other lens. It was for Ben, for his ballast. If I could get past the machines, Ben might too. He might attach Liam's humanity back to him, like Peter Pan's shadow, despite all the rest.

"He was brave, sunshine. He was your lovely brother. Look at his hair! It was just like yours."

"We would have played tricks on everybody," he says, smiling and leaning his head on my shoulder as we gaze at the screen.

· · · · · · · ·

The practice of visual art is not only in what we show, but in what we take away. A photographer sees things in the frame that don't add to the composition (or that detract from it), and she makes it disappear—diminishes it into shadow, changes her position, abstracts with shallow depth of field. An Alex Colville painting or a Mapplethorpe portrait have space inside them, brave empty space, and it sends our gaze to exactly where the artist points. They not only show less, but they bask in the less, throwing the point into sharp relief. This is white space.

A snapshot of Liam's wholeness—my broken butterfly, pinned to a board—was too much in the frame. The story of him was drowned in the clutter of his ordeal. Wires and electrical leads swirled around him, a mask, blocking me. The fuzz on his shoulder blade; the IV tube taped to his hand, long fingers in a fist; his pinpricked heel. Focus took the rest away, making white space in his story. In his toes, I could imagine who he might have been. This is how he became a boy to me. Piece by piece, wordless poem by wordless poem.

· · · · · · · ·

"I talk to my Jen's spirit everywhere in nature," said Muriel, her mother. "I stare at the sky and say *I love you*. I see her as a new form of energy. Know what I mean?"

Yes.

Not everyone is willing to talk about it, and so not everyone is kin. The death cooties. The thuggery of the forcible bootstrap pullers, the silent shoe starers, the my-dog-died-so-I-know-how-you-feel-ers. But there are all kinds of kin who have never held a dead baby. People who carry an array of losses openly, generously, with warmth.

Bereaved parents of any measure become the same caricature of screwed-up cosmic mathematics. We are not supposed to outlive our children. Not if they're thirty-seven years old or six weeks. That Debbie Reynolds would get the news of Carrie Fisher being gone? The universe breaks a sacred contract. We do not approve. This is why you and me and Muriel and Debbie Reynolds, bless her, share this kaleidoscope with more people than we might think. What of someone else's pain would humble yours? What of their mixed blessings would you wish for? More time plus a more complicated burden of accumulated memory and separation? More to reconcile, more left unsaid, unresolved, unreckoned? More autonomy, more apparent control? More chances to have intervened, saved, affected outcomes? What makes you say *Imagine the grief of that . . .* as unimaginable next to yours? Others look at you and think the same.

Irene and Jess and Bon and Josh and Chris and so many others who held dead babies. Stephen, three weeks ago, in Jersey City. We are the flotilla. But with a broader view, the companionship of the bereft is everywhere.

"Most of the time, when I cry about Jen, I'm crying because she was in so much pain," said Nick, early on. "I'm crying for her mom and dad that they had to see her suffer. It's not so much that she's gone, though it is that. It's what she had to go through. Know what I mean?"

Yes.

It is wrong that Derek hit the moose, that my prom date died in the squad car of his dreams. It is wrong that a lovely couple in Edmonton spent eleven years giving everything they had to their son who would always die one day or perhaps the next—that he couldn't laugh, run, tell them what he thought about things. All the miscarriages of friends and the years of infertility of others are wrong too. The interventions and stress and slippages of hope, all tangled up in the same endeavor as ours: to try and have children. All the bodies not cooperating feels wrong, with shocking consequences of various degrees. It is wrong that we might get sick or struggle or be expelled by war from a place we loved. Wafaa's displacement is wrong. Her country's destruction is wrong, and the violent loss of her son.

We are the only animals who know death will take us from each other, yet we are the only ones who are shocked when it happens. Dismay is unique to us. The Buddhists devote every last wit to letting go of fair versus unfair. To make all this wrongness easier, they say, we're going to have to quit being so surprised by it.

After Jen died, Nick took a photo to the nurses. *I wanted them to see her as she was, during her life, and not just with cancer, during her death.* It was one of my portraits of her. She is standing on a wharf in white lace made by her sister. It is almost sunset, after the ceremony but before the dancing. She is rosy and beaming. I shot around his shoulder as she leaned in to him, her cheek touching his lapel, her eyes shining toward me. I remember hitting the shutter, and the little rush of knowing everything had conspired: my position, the breeze, the light, her transparent joy. *That'll be a great one.*

It is now on a bulletin board in a palliative care unit, most probably buried under the curled edges of other loved and lost ones in their prime along with cards of appreciation. Her face as all those kind people should have known it, not unconscious but full of promise, in still life.

· · · · · · · ·

The sum effect of finding kin: one plus one equals infinity. A grieving person finds another grieving person—someone they might not have otherwise considered, drowning as they were in their own private pitch black—and a little light takes root. In hushed voices by the salt cod two humans listen to one another, trading familiar unfairnesses and stirring the oxygen they share. It's happened to me countless times: on sidewalks, at birthday parties, in a hayloft with a plate of barbecue. It is a shorthand, a safety, a space. A consciousness of breath and held breath. The pressure is eased and the light comes in.

You may be a long way from caring about oxygen. You may be still bleeding and dazed in rubble. Or you may be a decade out, like me, thinking *Yeah, I've felt that before.* A deepening, softening, opening to people in pain, though I resent the means. Had my son lived, the world would have had more love in it. He would have received, offered, and generated love. He would have played, invented, and explored. He would have mastered a particular dish. He would have had his own favorite corny pranks, dance-in-the-kitchen songs, mountain peaks, dog-eared books, wallet photos of when he was young. He might have had his own children. He might have said to them, *You'll always feel better with a nap and a shower. Also, never nap with your pants on. That's not a proper nap. It's what my mom always told me, so now I'm telling you.*

With Liam's death, the world lacks the love he would have made. Buckets and heaps and afternoons full of it. Whole lineages full of it. And that's true. But the alternative? There would have been nothing of him. No implantation; no splitting of cells. No uterine kicks and thumb sucking and groping around to discover *Hey. There's another me in here.* The erasure of Liam never having been Liam—even for a moment—would have been more sad than his traumatic birth, his limited life, and our terrible loss of him.

That he was here at all made more love in the world. With him, there would have been more. But without him, there would be less. I ache with this surplus. The ache is how I know it exists.

CHAPTER TWELVE

Womangood

About the female state as we move forward. On beginning
to build a life again rather than just surviving it.

WHEN I was a kid, I had a Kate Greenaway peephole tunnel book that had been written and painted at the turn of
the last century. I would gently pull the front edge and with a
delightful *crick-crick-crick* the paper would unfold like accordion
bellows. The first layer offered one small circle through which to
look, and the rest of the layers staggered to form a 3-D diorama
in miniature. I peeked through the hole at garden parties, kittens
playing in hedgerows, and girls with baskets and bonnets with
wide ribbons.

Crick-crick-crick. The peephole was a golden ticket, a white
rabbit, a cupcake that said EAT ME. Never mind the debtor's
prisons and rampant disease; I wanted to go to a tea party in
1898. The paper tunnel was transportation.

Memories are like that. A collection of peephole tunnel books.
They are never flat.

Crick-crick-crick. I am asleep on a canvas deck chair in the sun,
my hair in wet braids. I am sprawled flat on my belly, my arms
tucked under me, a beach towel on top. There are marigolds in
the yard. Cheerful voices and the pouring of lemonade and the
spray of the sprinkler are a white noise. I am safe and loved, and
the air is warm.

Crick-crick-crick. I stand in a crowd at a high school dance.

I like somebody. He doesn't like me. It is 1988. The Pet Shop Boys are on a video screen. My boobs are little, and my hair is big. My sweater is tucked into my jeans. I am embarrassed. So embarrassed.

Crick-crick-crick. I am wearing a wedding dress. We are walking down a village road, led by a piper. People come out to their front steps to clap. *Pssst* somebody says. I turn around. He snaps a picture.

Crick-crick-crick. I am lying on the floor of our dining room. My first child is almost walking. It's one of those scramble-around-in-nothing-but-a-diaper days. We are both sloppy and stinky. He flops onto me. ADLEE-GOO. His face is in my face. Then his elbow, then a chubby foot. He squirms and I catch him, roaring, squeezing his thighs. He squeals with a spitty, blueberry-smeared face.

Crick-crick-crick. I am pregnant again with identical boys, hugely, taut under a blue shirt. Evan and I sit in the sand. He is two. He grabs fistfuls and the sun is warm, the sky and the sea twin sapphires. The water brushes up against the beach. I do not know yet that something is wrong.

Crick-crick-crick.

. . . .

I hate you, body. I want to be inside you like a room, and I want to smash everything in it. I want to see you in bits. I hate you. How could you do this to them? I hate you.

I know, said my body, as I was wheeled to the incubators.

. . . .

After the baby dies, checkout line magazines are newly incomprehensible.

"30 Hot Sex Tricks!"

"The Easy Flat Abs Workout You Can Do Anywhere!"

"Get the Epic Love You Deserve!"

Other women rejoice and fret over fifteen pounds gained or lost, split ends, affairs, scars, crooked noses, crooked lusts, streaks of gray, crushes, careers. But the baby died baby died baby died oh my god the baby died. The baby died. *My baby died.* The woman whose baby died was betrayed by her uterus. Her own body betrayed the life growing inside of it. The snakes on her head are screaming, in unison, all day and night, nonstop.

· · · · · · · ·

Womangood was a typo. The *g* was supposed to be an *h*, and this was supposed to be about the strangeness of feeding and washing and hydrating this body. Of decorating it, dressing it, walking around in it. Woman bad. Woman stuffed, fucked, kaput. Broken body, never mind the heart. Her only sex trick? Not crying during it, eventually, maybe.

"You have to let go of the guilt. You have to stop punishing yourself. It's not healthy. Why can't you let it go?" he had said. The father of my children, bless him, wanted his wife back.

"It's not like I wake up every morning and choose it," I replied. "Imagine you're driving through a blizzard, and you cross the center line and crash and I am killed, or one of the kids. And imagine for the rest of your life, they make you walk around with the wreck of the car fused to you and for the rest of your life you ARE that wreck. You'll be that wreck forever. You'll eat and walk and sleep and do everything until the end of your days surrounded by all this twisted metal and blood stains. You know it was the black ice, not you, that did it. But you were still the driver. You were the one behind the wheel, and you'll never forget it."

He nodded. What else could he do?

Of course I know it wasn't my fault. Stillbirth, miscarriage, prematurity, SIDS, accidents: nature's chaos, a short straw, nothing more. I know. You know. Of course. But for a while, when everything is still smoking and spitting, *I know, I know* is instinctually followed by the knee's twitch upon being hit with a rubber mallet:

But I should have known
I should have gone back to check
I should have been more careful
I should have called the doctor
I should have gone to the hospital
I didn't

It's a reflex. It can't be helped. It's what makes the leap between tolerating womanhood and making womanhood truly good again seem like an impassable ocean.

· · · · · · · ·

Fathers: my gender is the obvious caveat. I can only speak to the car-wreck body and how it feels to be the vessel. This didn't happen to the mother of your child. It happened inside her. Consider this a peephole tunnel book. Maybe it'll be detached enough from your baby's mother—from the trees of your forest—that you might see something you recognize.

You two might be miles apart. Light-years. Or you might be standing together, holding on with a hooked finger or a knee against a thigh, bracing one another. You might be staring into space in the same general direction, not saying much. That might be okay. Or it might not be okay. Who knows. People go on about how the marital statistics after loss aren't a happy sight. But they're not in any case, are they? Every partnership comes with its own peculiar mix of inside jokes, recurrent annoyances, unspoken contracts, body languages, patterns of intimacy, gaps in intimacy, hot sex tricks, and suitcases of inherited anguish and anxiety. When loss happened, all the bonds or chasms that already existed between you were electrified. The outcome depends on what was there to begin with. Not on some arbitrary loss = divorce myth.

Your baby died. For a time, there will be parts of her you can't seem to reach. And you may have no idea what you need, let alone what she needs. You might wish she would stop talking. You might wish you could stop thinking. Or vice versa. You might think you have to keep it together so she shouldn't have to. Or vice versa. You'll get explosively upset on her behalf. She'll make you explosively upset. You might swing far apart and then close together again, but fleetingly, until next time, like planets orbiting on a mobile of the Milky Way. You might wonder if it's possible to ever find your jokes again, let alone your sex tricks.

Never mind the typical stuff they say about how men handle it one way and women another. I've known women who never wanted to speak of it again. I've known men who wrote poetry and still do, a decade later. The only certainty is that at some point, you and your partner are likely to be out of sync, either a little or a lot. You'll need something she won't be able to give. She'll expect too much of you. You'll both raise flags that will be either broadly missed or misinterpreted by the other, and you may not have the energy to rephrase, clarify, be a grown-up, or remember all the rudimentals unique to the two of you. You'll be tired, wrapped up in your own pain. Extreme loneliness, claustrophobia, guilt, or panic will inhabit both of you in turn, sometimes unheeded and neglected by the other, sometimes more malignant than benign, and this will land with a squelch on a growing, steaming heap of relationship shit that will grow six heads, and it's going to live in your house. It'll be your very own Greek hydra of relationship shit. Except it's moving. And hungry. And has six heads. And it might eat you both alive.

"MAWAGE," says the Princess Bride's bishop. "MAWAGE,

that bwes-sed awangment! That dweam wiffin a dweam. And wuv, tru wuv, will fowwow you foweva . . . So TWASURE YOUR WUV."

You brush your teeth together. You dance rude in the kitchen and check each other's moles. Dick jokes and neck rubs and sick days with chicken soup and piles of snotty Kleenex. And a six-headed Greek shit monster. Your particular monster might be wearing a sandwich board that says BABY DEATH. Another couple's six-headed Greek shit-monster might be wearing a sandwich board that says ALCOHOLISM. Or GENERATIONAL PAIN RE: ABUSE. Or CANCER. Or BIPOLAR DIAGNOSIS. Can you turn your six-headed Greek shit monster into good, clean compost for a fresh batch of brand-new dick jokes and neck rubs? Sure. Absolutely. Ninety percent of the bereaved couples in my life are still fine and better than fine. It won't be one shit monster that tips you one way versus the other. Just keep checking your moles, for heaven's sake. And the dick jokes. Dick jokes are important.

· · · · · · · ·

Green and dewy and edible and nourishing things grow in shit, you know. That stinking heap is the very thumping heart of Mother Nature, the ambrosia of resilience. Money doesn't make the world go round. Poop does.

We are a funny bunch. People who have never experienced loss or poverty or disease or anything in particular lie there, staring into space, feeling invisible. People who have suffered ten times as much as you and I—whose sons were left bleeding in an Aleppo street—write off a miserable day with a vow to get more sleep. A woman whose baby died a few years ago cries, mortified, at the bank. She forgot to set up automatic bill payments and she's five times late on her credit card, penalized with the 25 percent interest rate reserved for delinquents. She is disorganized and hormonal. Her husband tells her she'll feel better if she washes her face. She does.

The third one was me. Yesterday.

My baby died, for chrissakes. I would never cry over a damned interest rate, says the spectral imprint of circa-2008 Kate. *Nothing else matters that much. I will never have that kind of emotional real estate again.*

But I do.

Any one of us can play the who-has-it-worse game, either to shame others or to shame ourselves for being so damned delicate. If you do, no matter what your stance, you are correct. Yes. Some other people have it worse. Sometimes that person is you. And yes. Sometimes, you're being silly. You're catastrophizing. Turn that umbrella upside down. Pennies from heaven. No matter what you are—mourning or oblivious, close to your family or far away, broke or abundant, single or married, beset with X number of other traumas or not—you will invent a six-headed shit monster for yourself. We are imaginative, ambitious, and ponderous creatures. We are quick to both suffer and perpetrate a broken heart.

Add to the chatter: Is what feels like a six-headed monster—stress / misfortune / loneliness / self-pity / hardship / woe—the truth? Or is it just a question of where you're standing? If the answer is a grumbled *Maybe*, take a deep breath. Get some more sleep. Drink more water. Try again tomorrow. If the answer is *Yes, this is all true, because my baby died*, take a deep breath. Get some more sleep. Drink more water. Try again tomorrow. See the rest of us in parallel.

· · · · · · · ·

This kid smells good.

In Calgary in a front yard swing with my friend's baby on my lap. I would have evaded it, had I been able to. But it was nice.

I might have liked to have had another . . .

There was no man in my life, not for a long time, and I was carting around truckloads of guilt and shame, so much shame, over the end of marriage. Any reflexive womb flutter could only be entertained as a daydream for some alternate-world version of me. An alternate Kate who was still married and not forty. And who didn't have an exploding belly—the placental abruption, the footnote on my chart that was overshadowed by the TTTS but a recurring danger if I'd ever tried again. *Could I have had another without endangering myself or losing another one? If I were . . . also . . . several years younger? And with someone? I guess not.* The moment I came to terms with babies, I came to terms with being finished with them for myself. Or who knows. Maybe, more honestly, I came to terms with babies because babies had become definitively impossible for me. Perhaps that's when they became safe territory again.

My social circle includes a cohort of bereaved parents near and far, a constant sounding board and soft place to land. As time passes, they are an array of life after recovery from every possible angle. After her first baby died suddenly at six weeks old, Jen said *No way. Never again. I have dreams about trying to get pregnant and wake up drenched in sweat and shaking. I can't do it. I will never do it. I can't risk going through that again.* Years later—it took years—I see a Facebook video of her rolling out a pirate ship she made for her two-year-old son's first Halloween. They both laugh and squeal. Fist in the air.

After a genetic condition caused her daughter to be born premature and die in the NICU, Saavi wrote to me: *We tried for so many years. She was our miracle, and she is gone.* They called her Ekaja, Hindu for "only child." They went to Panama, to a little beach only the locals know about, with fresh fish and cottages on stilts. Initially, it was an escape. It was what they needed. But they never left. They found a community and a joy they can't imagine leaving. It's hot and lush and a long way from everything she once knew. Being a long way from everything she once knew suits her. It lights her up. Fist in the air.

A subsequent baby is not a consolation prize. A big life change does not erase a missing baby. Subsequent marriages, businesses, dreams—nothing negates the loss. But the adventures, accomplishments, and developments that continue to unfold in life after loss will surprise you no matter what direction they take, what hopes they fulfill, or what unchartered paths they offer. They will add to you in a way that will make you so much more than everlost.

· · · · · · · ·

Jacqueline du Pré's 1962 performance of Fauré's Élégie in C Minor, op. 24 is the orchestral accompaniment to a silent film of human existence, a devotion of hope colliding with despair in loops and circles. A storm! Trees falling and guns blazing and all the failures and exclusions and corruptions and senselessness of us. One cello, one piano. Six minutes and forty-six seconds. The blind rage, the wailing. The certainty that you will always be bristling with sadness. The fear of the everlost. The drifting of the present becoming the past.

We lament. This is our requiem, our composition for the repose of the souls of the dead. We wish for them to be tranquil, if we cannot be. *Sorrow* has as many synonyms as the Inuit do for *snow*, and it wraps around us as much as the white of the Arctic.

> What is a poet? An unhappy man who hides deep anguish in his heart, but whose lips are so formed that when the sigh and cry pass through them, it sounds like lovely music. . . . And people flock around the poet and

say: "Sing again soon"—that is, "May new sufferings torment your soul but your lips be fashioned as before, for the cry would only frighten us, but the music, that is blissful."

—Søren Kierkegaard, *Either/Or*

Fauré's Élégie in C Minor will make you cry, but exquisitely. It ends with a whisper. After, you'll feel clean. Someone else has known this pain. They must have, to have orchestrated sounds like that. You are not alone. Neither am I. Neither was Fauré or du Pré. It's not the music that is bliss. It's the companionship within it. On the same album, after the Élégie, is "The Swan" by Saint-Saëns—peace creeping in again, like Carl Sandburg's fog coming on little cat feet. We are sad, but calm. The Élégie would be less without the swan, and the swan less without the Élégie. They are as much a pair as a left hand and a right.

How do I get up in the morning and make myself breakfast when my baby is gone? It's obscene to butter a bagel when my baby is gone.

In the beginning, it feels impossible to get through the day without thinking about it (you will). It feels impossible to ever revel sexually in the body that failed you (you will). It feels impossible to laugh at a joke, let alone make one (you will). It feels impossible to ever be generative again, the highest echelon of being okay. Productivity. Imagination. The creation and invention of new things, new chapters and movements in your life. To not just reach the baseline of a moderately even existence but feel terrific about something. Big generative and small generative. Satisfaction, pride, spark. It's not impossible. It's inevitable.

You will never be yourself again. Not in the way you think of "yourself" as a concept. You will always be a bereaved parent. You will always long for what you have lost. But you will also be countless other things you don't know about yet.

It's okay to feel like this is impossible for you. You might even hope it's impossible. It may be too much to contemplate. That's okay too.

I feel sadness that Liam was my last. I feel gratitude, too. I am humbled by all those who tried again, who went through conception and pregnancy and labor after loss. I still look at them as some of the bravest people I know. I feel the same about parents who lost their only child and went on to invent unexpected lives down other, unexpected paths.

Okay, baby.

* * * * * * * *

A Fata Morgana is a mirage seen right above the horizon at sea. Ancient ships in the Strait of Messina attributed the optical phenomenon to Arthurian sorceress Morgan le Fay, seeing them as fairy castles or false lands to lure sailors to their deaths.

It will be some time before you worry about credit card debt, over-browned tourtiere, your crap boss, or commute traffic. It will be longer before you sit mindlessly in front of *Beverly Hills Cop III*. Vanity and slovenly peace are distant shores, and you will inch toward them with ripped sails, an empty belly, and sunken cheeks. But not until after you have spent the requisite time being at sea.

The first time you sense the ordinary woman of you on your horizon, she won't be real. She will be an optical illusion, your Fata Morgana. You won't be ready yet for everyday worries, despite wanting them (and not wanting them at all). The maybe-land woman you see, if you squint, is a trick of light and refraction. You will sail toward her anyway, just in case, and as you advance she will draw back to reveal more empty waves.

Until, one day, you will feel the lurch of sand under your hull.

* * * * * * * *

Are you still here, body?

Years later. I have not been kind. I have turned myself inside out. I have deprived myself of sleep, water, intimacy. *I am sorry. You tried.*

I did, says my body.

. . . .

When a word feels like a hinge, I look it up. Dictionary poem:

FALL

Be born, little lamb.
Come down freely under gravity
To lower or less upright, suddenly
Wounded or dead in battle.
Come to rest, settle or
Be cast down.
Diminish in pitch, volume, value,
Morality, chastity.
Pass into, give in to sin.
Lose primordial innocence
And happiness.
Be given inheritance,
Retreat from established course.
Cut down, drift off, give ground.
Lag unnoticed, neglected, unchecked.
Feel love for; be in love.
Be deceived or swindled by
Autumn.

. . . .

Mussels with coconut milk, fish sauce, lemongrass, red curry. Asparagus and crumpets. Slathers of stuff. Tempeh crumbled up and packed, pan fried, slathered. Long sourdough bread, slathered. *God, I'm slathered*, I wrote in my journal in the dark space after my marriage dissolved. *It sounds like exhaustion but feels like decadence.* I would put the little red table out and sit with my legs crossed with a dish towel on my lap. A buttery spread for one. I would eat and process photographs from weddings (see also: masochism); eat and look a while longer at that thing that was due; eat and write children's picture books. Silky poached eggs, spinach, mushrooms. Lentils cooked all day long with tomato and oregano and marsala wine. I would catch my reflection in the laptop and wonder: *Is this what I really am? Sitting here with my legs crossed, buttery, by myself and not minding it, at least mostly? Unluckily lucky?*

I was on my own for what felt like a long time. I needed to be, though the fear solitude would stick forever was a crippling one. *Some people*, I rationalized, *are with people because they're afraid of not being with people. That will never be me. I would rather be alone and learn how to be fine.* Some might have seen my little red table and sighed, imagining an autonomy that felt impossible for them. Others walked by holding hands and talking in quiet voices. Their symbiosis felt impossible for me. Sometimes I got up to look out my window. Sometimes I didn't.

I bought a six-inch cast-iron skillet. When the kids went to be with their dad and the empty house throbbed with emptiness, I cooked in miniature. If you can feed yourself well, you will always be alright. You have all you need to make yourself feel loved no matter what. Even if it's just you loving yourself. That's what my mother has always said.

· · · · · · · · ·

Marshall was a pirate. He painted my old crooked house. He had two teeth I could see, and his bones jutted out the back of his T-shirt. Everywhere he walked, he looked like he was walking uphill. I tried not to stare, but he had leathery skin, all grooved and burnished, and it made me stare. I wondered how old he was. He couldn't read or write. He poked at hornet nests and called them nasty little buggers and brought me outside to show me the papery remains. The torn-down houses of nasty little buggers alongside paint flecks in crabgrass, mounds of it with slivers of rotten wood, the collateral damage of creeping meadow on hundred-year-old shingles. Marshall smiled wide and laughed. It's what he did when he said hello or goodbye.

He did the first new patch of paint. Not so buttery, like it looked on the stick. More like butter-colored Crisco, the stuff my mom curses at when she buys it accidentally. Dyed to look wholesome, pretending.

"That's Some Yellow!" said Marshall in that south shore way, with equal emphasis on all three words, going up at the end and then down again, amused.

My house would be the color of butter-colored Crisco.

My dad's hammer banged new shingles, and Marshall scraped and painted. *Scrape-scrape-scrape. Knock-knock.* I walked across weedy grass with the crowbar. It was a fixing up of the only facade I could affect. Thanks to them, it would be yellow.

. . . .

By the time I grazed my scar with my fingertips, noticing the bumpity-bump as an afterthought, as a silvery line that was one of several accumulated features upon my landscape, it was no longer a crime scene. But that took time. Years.

You might never know what happened in this body. To see me at some reception or potluck, or even without clothes, almost nothing would be out of the ordinary. What you might know of me might amount to *The writer who lives by the little creek. She had a short film festival in the woods, on a sheet hung between two trees. She always makes the fire too big. She puts gorgonzola on pizza. She goes to schools and reads silly monster poetry to children, talks to high school kids about how art is a superpower. Lives with a storyboard artist, the tall funny guy. Yellow house. Two kids. Boys.*

Ten years after he died, whole swaths of people in my life don't know what happened or what life I had before. It's like having met somebody three or four times, chatting in aisles or at parties or on the sidewalk. You know some of the same people. And you've met them too often to back up and say, *I'm sorry, but what was your name again?* You've missed your moment. There are people in my life I've been friends with for a year or more. One in particular is having a Halloween party. I might go as Relic from *The Beachcombers*. Low-hanging fruit, I told her, and we cracked up. She doesn't know I didn't just have two kids. I had three. But I've missed the moment.

What's significant is that it might take me a year or more to realize you don't know. I might whisper his name into whatever room I'm standing in, into the hum of people talking and laughing, of drizzle outside and kindling crackling. And I might decide it's okay that you don't know. There is no *shouldn't*. I'm not resisting an urge to tell you. I don't have the urge in the first place. He is mine, integrated. I whisper him into the hum, and that's enough.

. . . .

My friend Elaine shared a "How to Recognize (and Escape) a Rip Current" infographic. *How did I not know this? I live in California*, she commented, as I, a Nova Scotian, thought the same thing.

When you're caught in a riptide—being pulled away from the land, into deeper water—don't try to swim against it. You will only exhaust yourself. That's how people drown. Don't panic. Float. Relax. When you feel it start to ease, swim across the current, parallel to the shore. Rip currents are a linear phenomena, columns perpendicular to the sand. They're narrow. They are not the whole beach. Just a sliver of it. Once you're off the rip and into normal currents, the waves will push you back to safety.

Don't panic. Float. Relax. Then, gentle. A little counterintuitive—not *to* safety, but alongside it, skirting it. Diminish in pitch, volume, value, morality, chastity. Lose primordial innocence and happiness. Wait. Give a little push, then drift. Wait a bit more. Then try again.

. . . .

Are you still here, body? Years later. *I'm sorry. You've been alright. More than alright. You have bumps and lumps but I'm glad to have you. I know I haven't been the easiest occupant. I'm a pain in the ass. Your ass. My ass.*

Only when you eat onion rings, says my body. *Forget about it. I don't hang on to stuff. I haven't got the room. Neither do you.*

. . . .

Every pregnant woman I saw smiled and glowed while I stamped and snorted, eyes peeled back with fear like the only horse who smells the barn on fire. Couples had much the same effect.

I am calm now. I don't feel so leprous, so out of place in mixed company. My apocalyptic visions are muzzled. I've seen, thanks to sheer numbers, that most of the time, the vast majority of everyone else will be fine, thank goodness. And I'm not angry about that anymore. Thank goodness. Time is all. Just time.

. . . .

June 14, 2016. It is the night before we go together to the lodge to canoe to Liam's tree. I am sitting with a gin lemonade, painting my nails on the front stoop. I am engaged. Nick shakes a shrieking Ben upside down like he's a pickpocket. Evan comes outside in his pajamas. They play ball hockey as a lazy, golden sun goes down.

Nine years ago, Liam was alive. Nine years ago tonight we took away the ventilator.

The thought hangs in the air. The boys send the ball careening into the front field. Hockey turns into a wrestle. Two monkeys stuff grass down a tall man's shirt.

Nine years ago tomorrow morning, Mother Nature had taken him back.

I try to imagine three. I can't. I listen for his voice and hear nothing but seagulls and wind in the trees. We are too far down a different path from the moment he left us.

I love you, baby. I wanted you. I miss you still.

"Aah! Aah! Let me go! Uncle! Uncle!"

Nick has Evan in a head lock. Evan is squirming and beaming, stars in his eyes. Ben runs circles around them, shouting NICK IS WEIRD HA HA.

Getting here was counterintuitive. I diminished in pitch, volume, value, morality, chastity. I lost primordial innocence and happiness. I waited. I gave a little push, then drifted, waited a bit more. I did not find a fairy castle. I built one, when I was ready.

So will you.

. . . .

Mommy.

(We were in the dark.)

The kids at school say I have an imaginary friend. I tell them Liam is not imaginary. I tell them he's in all the leaves on all the trees and the sunshine and the grass and the fish. I tell them if he was here he would be in my class, and I would sit next to him and he would sit next to me. We would be just the same.

You know what, Ben? Imaginary friends are just as important

as real friends. If that's what they think Liam is, it's really alright. Even if you feel like he's more.

You know what else, Mommy?

Yes, love?

I think we should thank Liam.

For what, sweetness?

(His whisper became whisperier.)

For giving his birth to us.

Oh yes, baby. We are lucky we had him with us for a little while. It was sad too, but you know what he is, right now?

What?

He's okay. He's just not here.

I wish he were here.

Me too, love.

(We were quiet for a while.)

Mommy?

Yes, love?

When me and Liam came out of your belly, what were we wearing?

Little purple suits and bright red socks.

(He giggled.)

Did we match?

Of course!

Mommy?

Yes, love?

What's an Eggo waffle?

Frozen.

What is moose poop called?

Moose poop.

(We were quiet for a while.)

. . . .

Love to the mothers with the undrunk milk.

Love to the fathers who had counted on things fathers should be able to count on: shoulder rides and Sunday pancakes. Love to the fathers who worry about her.

Love to the parents who have lived with grief for a while now, and who have adapted, mostly, but who still have no answers.

Love to the grandmothers and grandfathers who had been looking forward to so much, and who then had to witness the pain of their children in addition to loss.

Love to the brothers and sisters. Even though we're all grown-ups—we're supposed to know the why of things—we don't understand, either. Let's just keep getting muddy together. Somehow, I think that helps.

Love to the friends who couldn't find the right words, but who sat with us anyway.

Love to all those who couldn't—or wouldn't—sit with us, and who turned away in discomfort. Their own histories and fears were, for the moment, overwhelming. Forgiveness is a lifelong practice.

Love to the babies. *He is with mother nature,* I say. *She feeds him chocolate and lets him stir the sea and tap cracks in ready raven eggs. She lets him stay up all night long on sheepskins until he drifts off to laughter and wood smoke.*

Love to me, love to you. Forgiveness is a lifelong practice.